Also by Pastor Keyworth N. Ngosa

THE MYSTERY OF LAWLESSNESS-The Final Dimension

SATAN'S BEST KEPT SECRETS

His Nefarious Schemes & Deepest Fears Unveiled

PASTOR KEYWORTH N. NGOSA

iUniverse, Inc.
Bloomington

SATAN'S BEST KEPT SECRETS
His Nefarious Schemes & Deepest Fears Unveiled

iUniverse books may be ordered through booksellers or by contacting:

iUniverse
1663 Liberty Drive
Bloomington, IN 47403
www.iuniverse.com
1-800-Authors (1-800-288-4677)

ISBN: 978-1-4620-2933-4 (sc)
ISBN: 978-1-4620-2934-1 (e)

Cover Design: Pastor Keyworth N. Ngosa

Printed in the United States of America

iUniverse rev. date: 10/06/2011

To
Aishebo
(Aisha & Shebo)
I could not think of a better gift for our many years of friendship
You must fully understand God's ultimate purpose & love
for you. Your knowledge of this is Satan's worst
nightmare. His best kept secrets are
at your fingertips now

CONTENTS

ACKNOWLEDGEMENTS

The fact that a book bears only one name on the cover, does not tell the full story about who really labored to bring the work to life.

Hard working, faithful and effective people teamed up, each contributing a significant touch, without which, Satan's Best Kept Secrets would still be nothing, but a mere fairy tale.

All your hard and wise work has paid off, Mr. Patson Chifumbe (Americano); Mr. Hyginus M. Muyeleka, I salute you; Mr. Simon Njelemba, you have been an anchor; Gloria Hadassah Cross; Pastor Lawrence Mulando, thank you for believing in this work; Capt. Oggy Samatemba; Mrs. Chilala Watai; Br. Zali Chikuba; James Mwela (Lende), you have always been a great blessing since creation; Faith Ngosa, thank you little giant; Br. Joseph Tembo, your priceless encouragement I will always treasure; and Keyworth N. Ngosa Jnr., you typed two words. Masuzyo Ndlovu, thank you 'boyi'; Br. Joseph Siwo, you impelled me to greater heights; Rev. Leyton Hamvula Mulele, we've come a long way; Chungu Kapembwa, thank you very much for your priceless help; Pravin M. Patel and Mrs Isabel Deane (Barbados), godsends, I sincerely thank you for your timely assistance; Carol (Lanji) Lungu God always has something better for those who are faithful, you make me proud, thank you Angel of mice (John white). Mumsie (Mrs L.Kuyewana), luitumezi (little maize?). I heartily acknowledge the wonderful and hard working team at Iuniverse (USA); Randall, Faith, Jessie, Amy, Susan, Megan, Shawn, and the editorial team. And Mary Ngosa——this is it, it will lead us...

Nothing could have been done without this wonderful team. Thank you to everyone. I cannot repay you for the priceless help you have rendered, but...

Know that, He who takes note of the work of the righteous, has not forgotten you, even as His Word declares,

> Hebrews 6:10 "For God is not unrighteous to forget your work and labour of love, which ye have shown toward his name, in that ye have ministered to the saints, and do minister."

Rest assured He is faithful to put that to your account. And may His grace abound towards you more and more and may He fill your life with real success.

'**S**atan's Best Kept Secrets' is your selfless sacrifice, sweat, tears, prayers and desires molded in the Master's Holy, Life Giving Artistic Hands. The message is His, but I can joyfully say, you all are His messengers, just as I am. **THANKS**.

INTRODUCTION

It is with a joyful heart that I put down these words on paper to annihilate every lie of Satan concerning you. Discover who Satan was, who he is now, and who you are going to be, if you first grasp the importance of having a biblical perspective...

Now is your opportunity to understand the cover-up that Satan, a master of secret societies, has crafted over the years, which even his closest confidants are ignorant of. May this be your turning point.

The Lord gave me a vision in 1994; it was to become my turning point. I saw a long queue. People were falling into a gorge! In the vision I asked, 'What is this?' The Lord said, 'Those who are going this way will never return. All the people in that queue are going into the gorge. This is the way to destruction. I want you to help your nation, Zambia. If you go to the university, you will help yourself and your family. If you don't, you will help yourself and your nation. I will show you the operations of the kingdom of darkness and how to fight using the Bible.' Two years later I had a supernatural encounter that took me into understanding the operations of the spiritual kingdoms. On the 12th February 1996, the Holy Spirit took me into 'The Holy Spirit School.' For six months I never slept even for one second. I was awake 24/7. During that time my prayers ranged from 6-26hours. I learnt a lot about the spiritual kingdoms—God's kingdom and Satan's kingdom. And from that moment, I feel God's presence. Satan has done all he could to take me out. He has failed. As usual. Nobody is taking me out before my assignment is over. No body. In February 1998, the Holy Spirit said, 'From now, you will understand the Word as you read.' I have spent countless hours in studying the Word since.

Reading up on a certain topic, I gleaned some very interesting gems. When I first saw these gems in the Bible, I could not preach them. I thought I was going overboard, but it continued burning in my spirit. I just shared with a few brethren until I heard part of it from another pastor...to whom I am greatly indebted for the courage to put down the full message in print finally. You do not read this message like a newspaper. Meditate on it. If this message is true...if it is really God's Ultimate Purpose for you and I believe the Bible says so, then...

One, I assure you, can never be ordinary again after reading this message.

Keyworth N. Ngosa

Luke 8:17 *For all that is secret will eventually be brought into the open, and everything that is concealed will be brought to light and made known to all.*
(NLT)

1.

BIBLICAL PERCEPTION

Amos 7:8 *"...What do you see...?"* (NIV)

AMOS and the prophet Jeremiah were asked, by God Almighty, a simple but very important and demanding question, *'What do you see?'* You are being asked the same question today. As an individual there is a way you view life. You have a certain angle from which you look at it, your perspective. Perspective is the position from which someone views or looks at something.

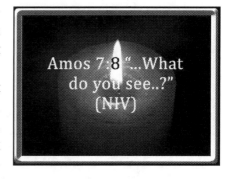

Perspective is the greatest difference between glory and gloom. When you look at life, what do you really see? Look at the headlines: pain, desperation, confusion and death are everywhere. Even the most elite scholar does not understand how this mess could be unraveled. It is this limitation that has made man realize, our solutions are not all here. We must appeal to something beyond our sphere. Friend, do not let your perspective be confined to the physical world. I would like you to know that there is another world. An invisible world. It is supernatural. In fact, there are two invisible worlds. *We are not alone.* Is what you see the real thing? Or is there more than meets the naked eye?

By having a broader perspective, you will realize that many people have tapped into the supernatural world. For example, some use Ouija boards, which mean 'yes yes' boards, astral travel—the common thing now, crystal balls to get into one of these two supernatural worlds, the devil's world. Do you think things like astrology—the horoscopes you see every day in newspapers and on TV are for nothing? The horoscopes—those zodiac signs, are a **direct express train** to the spirit world. What about yoga? The various astral planes it takes you to, friend, there is more to this life. And some secret societies, what are they really about? *No, they are just social clubs we are told.* Social what? *Clubs.* Halleluiah. Some of these secret societies are not as innocent as they look, their purpose is to connect you to the kingdom of darkness. **Many are in contact with the spirit world today, and you may be the only person on planet earth neck–deep in ignorance**. Do not be ignorant. Nothing is as costly as ignorance.

I. MODERN PERCEPTION

Beloved, I am a curious creature. I ask questions. I remember a day when I sat in my cozy seat and flicked on the TV. I made myself a good cup of cocoa and returned to relax. I had heard a lot about this film, Passion of The Christ. How it has blessed many. I didn't want to miss it for anything! People have wept to show how powerful the message is. I was ecstatic. The LG logo or symbol was busy darting on the screen. I pushed in my film, Passion of the Christ. As the film started, I noticed the ICON Productions logo. Then as the film progressed, my curiosity got the better of me, especially after noticing the film was way out of the Bible. *Wait a minute Keyworth. The film producer's logo, Icon, had one eye*. The LG symbol or logo is a face with just *one eye*. I am allergic to coincidences. *What is going on?* As I watched the film, Passion of The Christ, I saw more of the one eye thing—Jesus, had one eye. Is this film telling me what I am seeing or am I mistaken? Jesus has lost one eye? What does that remind me of? Horus. Horus is the son of the supreme god, who loses an eye in the battle against Typhon the crocodile–pig monster! One eyed savior. Sounds familiar? Is this Passion of the Christ savior losing an eye in the fight against evil? Since Osiris *lives* through the son, does not that eye denote the all–seeing eye? *The All–Blind Eye is most appropriate.* Barabbas and the thief on the cross (who loses an eye after being gouged by a crow—that is also a message on its own, but we save it for another day) all had the one eye problem. And then lo and behold Jesus' buttocks are put on display as the film ends. That did it for me. *Pure devilish.* This film has many unbiblical things and we all herald it as gospel truth? Shocking. But there is something good to be said about the film though. **It has clearly exposed how much Christians, including the clergy have fallen from grace! Mike, I agree some people look for anything to attack the clergy. Demonic allegations and childish evidence have been paraded to magnify the short comings of God's own. I am not for that folly. That is not what I am talking about.**

Believe me, I know how tough ministry is. And I would be the most foolish thing on two legs if I am unnecessarily attacking my fellow soldiers in Christ. We all falter. That is clear. But the way we seem to be openly magnifying wickedness needs to be addressed. This is not simple stumbling, but shocking and open defiance of the Lord Jehovah! We cannot pull Jesus down and continue ranting like mad men that this is our King. We can't deny Jesus and continue being Christians. What kind of undiluted nonsense is that? Anything that has a whiff of Christianity is accepted without any checking. Bible study has been thrown out. Whatever we are told, we swallow. Most ministers of the Gospel have welcomed this film even when they know it is not Christian. It is not based on the four gospels, but on something else. There is a serious and constant reminder of the Eye of Providence or the All-Seeing Eye in this film! Look at this

- ✓ Jesus has an eye problem when he is hit in the face. He has one good eye—Left eye.

- ✓ One of the guards who was dragging Jesus had one good eye—Right eye.

- ✓ One of the two kids tormenting Judas has an eye problem just after biting him and sucking blood. One good eye—

Right eye

✓ As Jesus is presented for judgement, he is shown standing with the guard who has one eye, both of them have eye problems.

✓ Barabbas has an eye problem, one good eye—left eye.

✓ When Jesus is being scourged, a female Satan is seen gliding behind the priests. She stops, coincidentally on the guard with one eye.

✓ The thief who hails insults at Jesus has his right eye viciously gouged by a crow.

✓ **Now this blew my mind.** After these eye problems, at the end Jesus dies. Then? A **teardrop** from the **sky** hits the ground and causes an earthquake. This is one secret message that is beyond ordinary eyes. Is God the Father shedding a tear for His Son? Or is it **Wedjet**? The Egyptian sun god in the sky who sheds a tear!!! **Wedjet always appears with a tear! One tear! In the film only one tear fell. And what is wedjet if not the All-Seeing Eye?!!!**

My friend, what do you see? I know I have simplified wedjet. We save the details for another day. The point still remains: **Even the poorest of exegesis could not have produced Passion of The Christ from the four Gospels.** It is clearly extra biblical material, how do we embrace it the way we have done? And not just simple extra biblical material, but **DANGEROUS** extra biblical material! *Anyway, anything goes in global oneness.*

Christians in the main suffer from a dangerous disease called bad attitude. They do not read. They don't research. They do nothing! Why did God give them brains if they can't use them? I slotted in another movie, a great series, Eureka. What is the main purpose of these great scientific displays in Eureka? What is Global Dynamics about? Has man finally attained the enlightenment he has sought all these ages? Has he become a god, through science? And did I see a pyramid as the symbol for Global Dynamics? I paused the film. *Is this a Masonic pyramid or not?* Is there a similarity between this pyramid and the one on the US dollar? I asked myself. *I'll find out.* What about Lord of The Rings? What is the purpose? Need we mention The Book Of Enoch? What is the Book of Enoch? And which Enoch? For the Enoch of the underworld and our Enoch differ. The underworld has Enoch who is the founder of Jewish occultism. The biblical Enoch wasn't in the occult. And any book written by the true Enoch will not have some strange underlying messages. What we have in the Bible is enough. Let's not be carried away by sweet discoveries, as harmless as some of them may appear. Many films nowadays have a strange theme that smolders beneath. Is it the reason now we have edutainment not entertainment? Are we being educated, in a subtle way?

Charles, do I talk about the Big Brother programme, which has taken us by storm, as Christians? It has an eye issue. **What is or who is Big Brother?** The real Big Brother is the reference to the eye of Osiris who watches constantly over his sister Isis. This eye watches over everything that occurs in the spirit world and on earth. That is the real background of big brother, not what we are told. This eye symbol is now everywhere. Time would fail me if I touched the music industry, the eye and the pyramid symbols have dominated. Strange symbols in music videos and films. The eye and the pyramid being prominent even there. Christian books (allow me to digress a bit here). The Bible. I am not saying anything here I am just thinking aloud, be the judge. I would like to show you a scripture.

Matthew 6:10 *Thy kingdom come. Thy will be done in earth, as it is in heaven.*

Matthew 6:10 *Set the world right; Do what's best—as above, so below.*
(The Message)

There appears to be some similarity between these scriptures, but I seem to have a problem because the words 'as above, so below' are of occult origin—Hermeticism. This comes from the grand master of occultism, Hermes who is believed to have lived in the times of Abraham. Did the translator pick these words out of innocence, not knowing what lay beneath? At first glance there is nothing wrong. But understanding the real meaning of 'as above, so below' is what is disturbing. To make the short story shorter 'as above, so below' is an **occult** term and it is also called the Law of Correspondence! This is a reference to **all things working in the Satanic New World Order!** It is the Romans 8:28 of occultism. If you have seen their god Baphomet, he has given this sign—as above, so below. This 'as above so below' is an astonishingly big topic. For it touches on the Star of David. In the occult, there is a reference to the star of the fallen Solomon or the double triangle of Solomon.

This 'star' has two triangles, one pointing up, the other below. Some contend, this is what is referred to as the Star of David! If they are not the same thing, then they are abnormally identical without any difference! And it is interesting to see that on the American dollar there is this 'As above, so below,' Star of David. Just on top of the *eagle*. And that is not all. Go to yoga. The star of David is there. Who is fooling who, here? The devil's own believe, Satan will one day rule the universe and God will be over thrown. And all his people will rule with him. That is another meaning of as above, so below, which they proudly and shamelessly parade on their money. What is interesting also is that this phrase or maxim is the root of satanic positive thinking. The average person doesn't know the difference between satanic inspired thinking and Christian thinking. This positive thinking, which has nothing to do with *self value* placed on you by the blood of Jesus Christ of Nazareth, The Son Of The True God, Jehovah,

> To make the short story shorter 'as above, so below' is an occult term and it is also called the Law of Correspondence

drives people to self realization or higher consciousness. Higher consciousness ultimately leads to becoming a god! We must tread carefully with the **'we are gods teaching.' (For this 'we are gods teaching' borders on Kabbalah evolution). As we teach lets caution the people about the kingdom of Satan's teaching on this too.** They tell you to think and continue believing, in a satanic or magical way and you will have your desire. I am a man of faith. I know the difference between this kind of believing and the Christian believing! It is unfortunate that phrase finds itself in the Bible...

Couldn't they have rephrased it? Great question Vince. How could they have picked a prominent or common occult phrase? What is worse, there are so many hermetic writings coming from pulpits disguised as the Word of God! Many sermons today have this coating. Esoteric teachings are being passed on to the people and how they gobble them with undiluted gluttonous appetite! Hmm. Let's get back to the one eye and triangle. Films and music are carrying this. **I am beginning to see a pattern.** There is a clear message coming to us from the screens. One just wonders whether it is a good message or a bad one. **Our friends have been told to make us comfortable with their symbols until we worship what they worship.** As I researched further I came to learn that this eye is *the eye of God* and some quote scriptures which they wrest to have a connection to the explanation. One such scripture is

Psalm 11:4 *The LORD is in His holy temple,*
The LORD'S throne is in heaven; His
eyes behold, His eyelids test
the sons of men.
(NKJV)

I don't see any connection between this scripture and an eye in a triangle! But they tell us the word 'eyes' in Hebrew is singular, so it is the eye of Osiris. The Biblical God is the same as Osiris. Wait a minute sir. They are not the same! We know this eye is referred to in Freemasonry as the All–seeing eye. In Hinduism it's the third eye of clairvoyance. And in Egypt's religion of Light, it is the eye of Osiris. It has nothing to do with the biblical God. Nothing. We are told the eye and the triangle represent the TRIUNE GOD. The three in one God. Which three-in-one god? The eternal triangle of god they call it. And have you noticed, dear, that these eyes sometimes alternate? Right eye and left eye? Any special meaning? When you see the right eye, it is Osiris—Satan (the sun god) they are referring to. The left? Good guess. Isis, Satan's deputy (the moon god or goddess) they refer to. *There is nothing evil about it, we are told.* Perspective. What do you really see?

Christianity offers the greatest and blessed perspective. **And the path that leads us to this blessed perspective is the Bible.** The Bible is a supernatural book. Believe it or not. The two worlds of the supernatural are revealed in the Bible. The more you learn from the Bible the more you realize you can never be neutral. It is either one or the other. But the Bible without the Holy Spirit is not enough. I used to read the Bible very much; sometimes I could finish the entire New Testament in a day! But things wouldn't just click. I read books and books, but all that ended in my information tray. I got something, but not the real thing my heart wanted. But in February 1998, *scales* fell from my eyes and I began to understand what my intellectual mind could not comprehend. Do not just read books and remain excited without the revelation from the Holy Spirit, it will not help you. I have seen people with head knowledge and no Spirit knowledge. A pitiful sight. They jump and howl, but when it all settles they realize they do not have it. **When the Holy Spirit has revealed something to you, your whole being holds on to it.** *Oh, our friends also have* **The Holy Spirit.** *Beware!* The revelation from the true Holy Spirit becomes part of you. It is something that even the hard tests of life fail to completely obliterate. No pain from the pit of hell will stop you. In fact it becomes your anchor to see you through during turbulent times. I would like you to fully understand the revelation in this book. Let this message sink into your spirit. Be prayerful and let the Holy Spirit open your eyes. The key that starts dismantling Satan's best kept secrets is *True Perspective*. Biblical Perspective.

Psalm 14:1 *The fool says in his heart, "There is no God."*
(NIV)

The person in this scripture is *the fool* because his sight is limited to the physical world alone. When one says there is no God, he also implies there is no devil. And in the absence of these two, there is no invisible world. That is being shallow. We have all trodden the path of the fool anyway. It is not what you say but what is really deep in your heart that counts. For some confess there is God, but live as if He never exists. It is common knowledge that evolution and its big bang counterpart nearly sent the Bible to the morgue. *God does not exist. The universe created itself.* But serious investigations have totally interred evolution and the sudden 'magical' appearance of the universe. Scientists have come to the conclusion that truly the world has a Creator. And these scientists are not all Christians. Interesting. After careful investigations, *evolution theory* has produced terrible defects that are inconsistent with the same science which it tries to use. Evolution is worse than abracadabra. You must have blind faith to believe in it.

Common sense, which I presume to be common, shows things on earth are being influenced by outside forces. Look around, a lot of supernatural activities are going on. You can try to put various guises or labels on them, but they still remain what they are, **supernatural**. These activities are coming from forces outside our world, believe it or not. The examples we gave earlier like astral travel are real things being done right now. You may not believe in them, but they are taking place in your backyard. Not believing in them does not negate their existence. As they say, you may be in deep denial. It is important to be aware of the supernatural worlds around us.

Decide today how your life will be. I decided to up my game some years ago. Only a handful of people know the real reasons I turned down the opportunity to go to the university to study Engineering or Mathematics, but instead opted to become a pastor. Apart from the clear direction from God, here is one of the other reasons. The year was 1994, a day in the month of September around 02:00am, sleep just evaporated from me and I became wide awake. Suddenly I saw a woman pass through the wall into the bedroom where I was. I sat upright. She was in white. Her eyes had no pupils. I came to learn later that she was the spiritual leader of a certain secret society. A friendly, humane society? She told me that she wanted me to stop being a Christian and abandon the vision of being a pastor. From that moment many people and strange circumstances have tried to take me away from the call. **The woman told me that 'they' were ready to offer me a lot of money and every form of material wealth I needed.** Before I could reply, a light flashed in the ceiling and just as it did that, the woman fled passing through the wall.

A voice thundered: If you want to give him anything, give him all that Jesus has to offer!

That voice I was to learn later is the voice of the Holy Spirit. Then the voice said to me: They have planned to kill you. **All this I experienced with my physical senses, my eyes and ears. I was wide awake. I was a Christian, but from that day I became a Christian!** No more games. The devil was real and God was real! Shortly I was approached, during the day, twice in that week and told off that **'They were going to block all my prayers from being answered'** and **'They were going to take away everything I owned'.** I have witnesses. In fact the brother I was with on one occasion asked me, 'How does this woman know you are a Christian?' Friend you are not hidden. They know you. All the people who approached me are big people in society, the woman who passed through the wall, the woman who told me my prayers would be blocked and the man who said I was going to lose all I owned if I did not quit being a Christian. I made up my mind; no matter the cost or pain, I was going into deeper commitment to Jesus. *If Christianity is fake why am I receiving this unnecessary attention?* I used to ask myself. For some time that *word* of losing seemed to hang on. Then the devil fell. And how great was his fall in my life. But one thing has remained etched in my spirit, the devil only comes in two ways

✓ To offer compromise

✓ To fight if you refuse compromise

Never settle for compromise. Never. It doesn't matter the pain, but whatever you do, compromise must never cross your mind. I have experienced the inexplicable in the supernatural. **I understand the supernatural kingdoms and their operations. I have been there. I am not writing this to convince you; SORRY I DON'T HAVE THE TIME!** I am just a messenger from Jesus to you. Take it or trash it. It's up to you. People who are still in Satanism have come to me in despair and poured out their deep secrets and how tired they are of The System. Some of them have paid dearly for that afterwards. And the devil, knowing that I know, has tried to unleash hell on me, but what he forgot is that this is a game at which two can play. He regrets having started it.

Delve into the world of the supernatural and see what is happening in the invisible worlds. Ouija boards, drugs, witchcraft, economic tricks, prostitution, questionable societies all lead you to Satan's kingdom, while the Bible leads you to God's kingdom. The truth you must know is that these two spiritual kingdoms have a direct impact or influence upon our kingdom, the earth. They decide what happens. Many are tottering under dejection and confusion reigns in their lives. They do not understand what is going on. Now you can understand. Demons have operated insidiously for a long time. Not anymore. **I would like to show you ways for courage to swell up in you.** Cowardice is not for you. Do you know that animals of prey view anything that runs away from them as dinner in the jungle? Cowards are the devil's dinner. Do not let sweat pour from every pore when you face Satan. He is not worth a drop of sweat.

Enter the supernatural world with me as we totally abandon our limited perception of life to a broader, and much challenging one. Are you ready to step into the supernatural and change what you see, totally? Here are some real people and real experiences in the supernatural. **Remember anyone who taps into the supernatural world becomes supernatural also.** Depending on the kingdom you are in, you function according to that kingdom. Your worldview may just never be the same again. And believe it or not what you have been seeing may not just be the real thing. Your limited perception may have just been costing you a lot. Let us look at real biblical characters, masters of perception, and how proper perception helped them in decisive moments.

II. MASTERS OF PERCEPTION

A. DAVID

> 1Samuel 17:33 *And Saul said to David, Thou art not able to go against this Philistine to fight with him: for thou art but a youth, and he a man of war from his youth.*

According to some Israelite tabloids' opinion polls and the PTV *(Philistine Television)*, David was much better off not poking his nose in affairs that did not concern him. David going into that fight was not even second favorite. He was a dead boy walking. A complete write off. It was only the Holy Bulletin *(From some serious Christians)* that published an article and I quote,

'If it is the Lord's will he may survive the giant's onslaught. But we are praying for rain to come and disrupt the fight so that our boy comes home without further damage.'

Their prayer was a prayer of damage limitation, not victory. David refused their opinion polls. He heard them but they never reached his heart. **What demonic perspective have you allowed to shake you to the roots?** A man who has really heard from God does not carry out a census before he obeys God. David was not moved by Goliath's Curriculum Vitae because Goliath had never fought a man with a CV like David's. Goliath had not challenged David or Israel, but the Almighty God. That is why when David looked at Goliath, he was filled with pity. He saw a giant funeral and felt for the pallbearers. But David's brother was incensed.

> 1Samuel 17:28 *But when David's oldest brother, Eliab, heard David talking to the men, he was angry. "What are you doing around here anyway?" he demanded. "What about those few sheep you're supposed to be taking care of? I know about your pride and deceit. You just want to see the battle!"²⁹ "What have I done now?" David replied. "I was only asking a question!"*
> (NLT)

Shame has a way of expressing itself. It may be disguised, but it still comes out. Eliab's problem was shame. Shame of being seen running away from the enemy at a stealth bomber's speed. Instead of accepting he was a coward, he labeled David

- ✓ Careless—he left the few sheep without a caretaker 1 Samuel 17:20

- ✓ Deceitful—he convinced himself David amplified his testimonies, to appear better than others. But that was not David's spirit, he was a humble boy, Eliab was lying. And besides, he just wanted to see how the battle was going while asking irrelevant questions as if he could do something about the situation.

✓ Proud—which he confirmed he had known about, thanks to the testimony of the bear and the lion

David was considered, unfortunately by his brethren, proud for saying Goliath would fall. On your way up you will be misunderstood until there is no word or grammar to describe it! But you don't care. **Listen, the Bible gives no room to apologize for our big mouths!** Read that again. 2 Corinthians 3:12 says that because of the great hope we have, we should be **bold** and not mince words. Understand that boldness is folly in the ears of many. Listen, I am a firm believer in the leading of the Spirit. But what I see nowadays is not waiting for the Spirit to lead, but cowardice. The only area we don't wait for the leading of the Spirit is in money making. Sow a seed. This is fertile church. All your problems will go if you give to God, the spirit has spoken. (This spirit only talks about money) And the minister gives you a book or a tape and you go home happy. Plundered. *What about sin?* Shh... keep quiet. That is destroying the faith of the beloved ones. Okay. I agree. Do we warn the people that their faith should go beyond believing God for bank accounts because very soon, they are going to realise they are pilgrims? The world system, which is designed to fail, will shock them. They must not have faith in it, only in God. *No, let's use wisdom.* P-l-e-a-s-e!!!

A Christian uses wisdom always, unless he switches off!!! Today's gospel has holes that evidently show a serious invasion and takeover. Are you going to be a spectator? Won't you contend for the faith? Can't you see what is going on? We have giants of well organised secret societies that have vowed to annihilate Christianity. They seem to have the capacity or the means. And we have seen what has happened to all who have opposed them. They pervade every sphere of life. These giants affect economies, politics, family values etc. And these giants have another gospel. For even our churches are totally taken over. You are the one God is counting on. The question is, are you going down in history and in the great book of God as a David who stood up and left a legacy or a coward who scampered leaving a plume of dust behind? When David saw Goliath, something in him was moved.

1. Spiritual Connection

All those insults from Goliath enraged David. He decided to do something about it. But like the intelligent people we are today, what do we do? Can I fight or wait? Can I do this or is it presumptuous? Standing orders are there, defend and confirm the Gospel. Some one cannot be insulting your family and you just sit doing nothing. You have the Spirit and it is clear that it is not by chance the giant has come out when you are there and everyone is fleeing. DO SOMETHING! *But Pastor Keyworth, it is not by might nor by power.* Good. That is why you should go and face Goliath now! *But... but... but.* Keep quiet Bat. It is not the stature of the opposition that counts, don't look at that. And never look at the enemy's face (some are very ugly—to scare you), look at the size of his shoulder. He may be big, but a corporal in rank. Davie was small, but good Lord, the boy was a live wire!!! He electrocuted Goliath. Thirty three thousand volts passed through Goliath. Goliath died in shock. David's brothers rebuked David. King Saul thought poverty was driving David to the edge.

Because of his offer,

> 1 Samuel 17:25b *...The king will give great wealth to the man who kills him. He will also give him his daughter in marriage and will exempt his father's family from taxes in Israel."*
>
> (NIV)

The king was convinced the poor boy was sacrificing himself. King Saul would have almost fired his commanders for bringing a kindergarten boy to him. King Saul's speech was crystal clear, 'I don't like jokes!'

> 1Samuel 17:33 *"Don't be ridiculous!" Saul replied. "There's no way you can fight this Philistine and possibly win! You're only a boy,*

and he's been a man of war
since his youth."
(NLT)

King Saul wanted to talk David out of the fight. Saul was behaving exactly like Peter, trying to talk Jesus out of His greatest opportunity in life. Don't you ever let anyone talk you out of your inheritance. That challenge that has plagued others for years is your passport to success. Yes that very thing that is making you feel like quitting Christianity is your key. Others may quit, but don't you dare even think about it! Others may have failed, but God has allowed it to come your way so that you defeat it. That is having a blessed perspective!!!. David refused to be moved by myopic perspective. You must also refuse. When King Saul had finished his speech, David gave him a side he had never known. David chased a lion and a bear, retrieved the sheep and when they charged at him he beat the living daylights out of them. No wonder he was called a warrior even when he was not in the army. David was a spiritual boy. He was no ordinary boy. That 17–year–old boy people disregarded had tapped into the supernatural in a way that many never knew. **Listen, some people think they know you, they don't.** They are in for undiluted shock!

Matthew 13:54 *He returned to Nazareth, his hometown. When he taught there in the*
synagogue, everyone was amazed and said, "Where does he get
this wisdom and the power to do miracles?" [55] *Then they scoffed,*
"He's just the carpenter's son, and we know Mary, his mother,
and his brothers—James, Joseph, Simon, and Judas. [56]
All his sisters live right here among us. Where did he learn all
these things?" [57] *And they were deeply offended and refused*
to believe in him. Then Jesus told them, "A prophet is
honored everywhere except in his own hometown and
among his own family." [58] *And so he did*
only a few miracles there because
of their unbelief.
(NLT)

They thought they knew Jesus but they didn't. When they realised they didn't know Him, they became offended. **How nice!** The Bible is clear, one who is born of the Spirit is unpredictable. John 3:8. When they realize you are not like them, they will do all they can to pull you down! Somebody who is born-again, not a poor imitation, is extraordinary. You may think you know him, but you don't. When David was taking on Goliath, he was not risking it all. Goliath was the one risking.

But Goliath, it must be mentioned, was not a simple person either. **He came from a nation that practiced witchcraft. Sorcery was the Philistines' national religion.**

Isaiah 2:6 *For You have forsaken Your people, the house of Jacob, Because they are filled with eastern ways; They are soothsayers like the Philistines, And they are pleased with the children of foreigners.*
(NKJV)

Isaiah 2:6 *For the LORD has rejected his people, the descendants of Jacob, because they have filled their land with practices from the East and with sorcerers, as the Philistines do.*
(NLT)

The Philistines were sorcerers. The night before the fight every witch and wizard in Philistine converged at Goliath's house. They did not want to become slaves. Chants and all forms of incantations were made. **What the ordinary person doesn't understand is that chants and incantations are prayers.** Not to God the Father of Jesus. To the devil. Listen, David the night before the fight was under heavy satanic bombardment. Curses of all kinds were unleashed on him. The battle ground was fully booby–trapped, for David to be defeated. But we know, curses will not cling to a worshipper. Never. If you worship God genuinely and consistently, stand your ground, you will see the salvation of the Lord. Friend, people saw two men, in fact a man and a boy getting ready to fight, but the reality wasn't so. It was two invisible kingdoms coming to a colossal collision. Goliath was neck-deep in the occult. Apart from his stature (2.7m to 3.3m) and skill, sorcery backed Goliath.

2. Sorcery & Technology

Brethren, sorcery, you must understand, is the manipulation of people, circumstances or events by demonic power to one's short–term advantage. Sorcery and religion blend. While religion is something acknowledged as good and sorcery as being bad, there is a point where they fuse. And to disguise sorcery, it now appears as technology in our times. Sorcery and technology can hardly be distinguished. **Most of our great technological advancements are greatly linked to sorcery**. Ladies and gentlemen, I don't stand to be corrected. In the name of advancement we see demonic engineered discoveries. Let's take cloning as an example. Some have good intentions and others are pursuing their father's nefarious schemes. Those pursuing evil ways will use organ donation to blind masses. Forget about the improvement of life by organ donation and the production of more food from animals! That's the passport to legitimacy! There are mainly four real reasons behind cloning;

- ✓ Beauty Products: Real warfare

- ✓ Food: Power and Worship

- ✓ Intelligence Gathering: Christian Traps

- ✓ Law Enforcement: Mind Controlled Assassins

Let's look at the first two points. Unfortunately we have to save the other two for another day. . .Not long ago, men were ecstatic about facing the chopping board. Circumcision had suddenly become the in-thing. We were given all the sweet reasons why the chopping board was the only solution for us to become real men. We were promised blissful sex. The main one was reduction of HIV/AIDS. And suddenly women wanted dudes without skins. The guys had to brave the doctor's blunt axe to feel manly. What I didn't understand was whether this was also going to make women HIV/AIDS resistant and have that fantasy-world sex. I am not against circumcision. It's there in the Bible. And in our culture as Luvales we proudly do it. That is fine. What I find mind blowing is this circumcision mad rush. Why? Thank God I didn't have to wait ages for reality to hit me in the face. It didn't take long before others began to cry foul. They had just discovered foreskins were a big issue on the market. The time we were all lining up to shed our skins (like snakes) there was a high demand somewhere for the same skins! Jesus Christ, we just got swindled! See how painful being blind could be? Ever heard of manufacture of consent? The manipulation of peoples' minds to make them accept some wicked scheme, which under normal circumstances the general populace can't accept? With the use of foreskins in facial creams, one has two think twice about our technology. Ignorance has shown that many are unaware of baby parts being used in various wicked industries. But thanks be to God not everyone is ignorant. Some people have risen to the occasion and said 'This is madness.' And to hush hush everyone who is against human parts' harvest, cloning is the answer. Harvest human parts, quietly. Fetal parts and placentas are being used in beauty products. What's the big deal anyway? When the devil looks at Christians, he sees them participating in rituals. The use of these products is not different from rituals. They may disguise witchcraft, but we can still easily see through it!

Believers are unknowingly participating in satanic rituals just like some people who take a piece of the body of their victim and sew it to their suit or put it in their lotion. This is an underworld formula for power. We know about these weird practices in Africa. People have been using lion, crocodile and human parts (skins) and putting in their lotions. Has anything changed? Just the labels and packaging. We have just added the label of science or technology. Nothing new, it is still witchcraft. Witchcraft is witchcraft, be it in Europe, Africa or Asia. Have you ever heard of Human to Product Technology? It is a lesson in advanced witchcraft that uses human parts into something human beings will use. But this is done by Satan's power. For example it's easy to turn a person into a cow. And people will innocently enjoy this meat, not knowing what it really is. I know this sounds abnormally extreme. Believe it or not, this is the world we live in. Many Christians have no idea who the devil they fight really is. The more you use such things, the more you are weakened spiritually. Please be prayerful before you buy things. Read on and you will know the role Isis plays in all this.

But for Christians you don't only become weak, it brings a demonic heaviness. Demons make you feel heavy as if you are carrying something. The Spirit of God makes you feel light. The spirit of heaviness is not a simple demon, wake up. Isaiah 61:3. It is serious bondage. Christians slowly begin to lose interest in real Christian issues. What excites the flesh is what they go for. In other words, this is spiritual warfare. Catch this by the Holy Spirit. 1 Corinthians 2:14. It is hard for the natural man to understand this. It sounds absurd. This is something that must be spiritually discerned. Brethren, our weapons are not carnal. Let's wake up. Be prayerful. We are being weakened so that when the enemy strikes we cannot resist. Yes, we have been told about these collagen products and how it is *mostly* animal collagen being used. Who doesn't know that animal collagen is not as good as human collagen? The devil just had to make sure it was human collagen! And most of it is usually **donated**. I love coincidences. We have collagen products for

- ✓ External use

- ✓ Injections

- ✓ Oral

Yes dear. Somehow it had to come to swallowing. Gross. In most cases we are left in wonder land. Is it cow, pig or human collagen? The devil would love us going for nothing less than human. **I know him**. I have sat long enough at the feet of the Holy Spirit to be ignorant of such schemes. So, whether someone claims to be doing it purely scientifically or not, the result is still the same. Demons capitalize on the use of human parts on our bodies, one way or the other. If your life just depends on the five senses, you are headed for disaster. Some things are spiritually discerned!

Brethren, **we are not ignorant of the devil's devices!** The Holy Spirit has trained us. What the Holy Spirit has taught me, no one will *unteach* it! I also know that cloning is to provide babies as food. *Human baby meat is tender!* Another weird solution from hell. The kingdom of darkness has been cloning since time immemorial. I am not talking stories here, but real life issues! Isis has been in the business long before we even knew the first letter of cloning. Human cloning is new to the kingdom of man, not the kingdom of darkness. Astral travel and cloning are very close relatives. There is a difference though. Surprised? Welcome to real life. There is this man who was a security officer. What puzzled his neighbor was that he was always at home but also at his work place in the night. His double or clone would be at work, while he is at home! And this has been a common practice for those in Satan's service. The neighbor, who was his superior at work, narrated this.

But that is not all. A man was lured somewhere by a friend. They got in the car and sped off. On their way they were involved in an accident. The man was badly injured. The friend who had invited him came out without a scratch. What shocked the people was that at the time of the accident, the same man who had invited the friend was spotted in another city! And people could prove it. This became a puzzle and some people called me over this same issue to find out how possible this is! It is an old system in Satanism—bilocation or multi-location. Usually it is impossible to kill these clones. Unless the original at home is dealt with. Has it not been said, and not sotto voce, that even Alphonsus Maria de Liguori could bilocate? Reality is stranger than fiction, to the common ear and eye.

Time would fail us if we looked at the lives of others like Most Venerable Mary of Agreda, who would move across the globe yet still home! The Holy Spirit does not give us ability to bilocate or transmute. We can see clearly under which spirit someone is operating. Most ordinary people we see have altars in their homes and are doing these things. Don't be fooled. Don't be fooled. Their ability to have these doubles or *clones*

comes from their altars of devil worship in their homes! Please understand I am not talking about these simple doubles made by plastic surgery. The devil has so many weird solutions for anything that blind men want. **And the devil is no respecter of persons, religious or not, we can all fall into his traps if we become careless.** Zedekiah thought he was beyond deceit. He actually punched Michaiah for telling the truth! The devil has another solution for diseases. What about the dreaded cancer? How far would you go in getting a cure? After all, there is no right (true) perspective or wrong perspective, thanks to Continuum Thinking. **As a woman, simply drink a man's semen. Let him ejaculate in your mouth. Look, it benefits you. Your cancer goes down. It's harmless protein. And it's birth control. You can't have it this great, not so Love?** Isis, the person many Christians are ignorant of and yet the whole world totters before her solutions, smiles with satisfaction.

But we know semen drinking has been a religious practice from ancient times. Men and women have been and **are** still drinking cum. Most people who are engaging in certain things do not have an idea what they are doing. But the devil does.

Friend, the devil is programming us. But do you see the **Trail of Depravity**? How did we find ourselves using fetuses as ingredients in our products? It's not by accident. We accepted *the fact* that we needed rights. Then those rights led to our kids doing whatever they wanted. And doing whatever they wanted led them to sleeping with anything they could find, animate and inanimate. On the other side, the main guys in the shadows were clapping. Our little pregnant daughters didn't want the bundles they were carrying. What did we do like the geniuses we are? We had to create more rights, for them to abort. And someone somewhere was interested in what they were aborting. And from that moment our daughters have been **donating** their merchandise! And the big guns would put these human parts in various products. Humanity just became cheap. Morals are loose and there is no restraint. When they come to church, they find Pastor Ngosa who tells them,

'God loves you. Don't feel bad, we are all sinners saved by grace. What you do is not bad. Just feel good about yourself. After all, Jesus is not the only way. So whatever makes you feel good, do it. Let your true self come out.'

We can't sit down like fools! Enough is enough. Look. We are not saying all of us we do something. If the devil is your dad, enjoy the moment. If he is not, come on board and contend for the Gospel of Jesus our true Savior. But many would rather bury their heads in sand like the proverbial ostrich. Yes the wicked today, like Goliath, are confident things are going their way. What they don't know is that all they will ever do is in vain...

Exodus 18: 11 *"Now I know that the LORD is greater than all the gods; for in the very thing in which they behaved proudly, He was above them."*
(NKJV)

Goliath was confident it was his day. But what this big baby did not know was that David, the small boy, was his acid test.

You are the enemy's acid test. Goliath was confident of the outcome. However, he was to learn later that one cannot take the Devil at his word. It has a 100% disaster record. There is a very important lesson to learn from David or Goliath though. You may think you know someone but you know absolutely nothing about him. **You do not know a person until you know his spiritual position.** Today there are many people, who are deeply rooted in the occult and these are the people we trust unquestioningly. Let's clap for ourselves. We are smart. You can never challenge a person in the occult outside Jesus. Never. There is only one reason why David could defeat Goliath, he had spiritual backing. The one in whose name David fought was the key; he mentioned that to the giant. **What name is backing you in the spirit kingdom?** Unfortunately this is one issue that demands your considered option.

Child of God, faith is not a risk. Faith is a certainty. You know what is coming. God rewards anyone who has confidence in Him. Suppose you make a mistake? God knows that your intention was for His good. He is not saddened by that. We do not worship a God who is ready to give you a thrashing immediately you stumble. God honors every step of faith you take. God is pleased by acts of faith. David was doing just that. If David had missed those five stones, we are talking about another conclusion, but God made sure there was only one outcome, Goliath's defeat. David released the stone and it sank in Goliath's forehead. I am often tempted to believe the stone hit him between the eyes, where his supposed third eye was. **David's faith was not in his great ability to sling, but in God**. God will never fail you. He will never. Some people wait for fire and lightning to come that's when they will move. Halleluiah. Keep on waiting, it will never happen. **You know what is right, do it!** It is true, the world today is almost inch by inch littered with devil worship. It is everywhere. Every sphere of life is under siege. **So, Christians let's see what you are made of.** The devil and his own have visible presence, what are you going to say? Yes it's true the entertainment industry, the political scenarios, the men of the cloth and even socially we see alarming levels of Satan's invasion. You cannot even tell who is teaching your children nowadays.

Dear Christian, there is no better moment like now. Stop whining and prove yourselves!!! We have our own Goliath today, and he is far much bigger than David's. Fight or fall. The Philistines had taken part of Israel's land and they wanted more than the land. They wanted slaves. It is not different today. Whether we like it or not, the world is on the brink of satanic slavery. The things people complain about, are part of the greatest nefarious scheme to bring the whole world into satanic slavery. Unsatisfactory political systems, unequal wealth distribution, economic hocus- pocus, religious madness, pastors and priests who are something else on pulpits and another thing in private moments—all these are just part of the big death web. I am talking about **hardcore Satan worshippers** who stand on the pulpits, misleading the unsuspecting masses! Men and women with hardened hearts. Men and women, dedicated to the total destruction of Christ and Christians. The devil will not leave you alone until you are his slave. Stop watching the devil take what belongs to you. He won't stop. He wants you to finally bow before him. You have two options, fight or fall before him. It is up to you. I'd rather die standing my ground than bowing before any monster. This was David's case. After taking part of Israel's land the philistines would come and provoke the Israelites. **Are you not tired of being pushed around?** The devil is looking for a fight, don't disappoint him, **GIVE HIM ONE!!! One he will never ever forget.**

David picked five stones to deal with the giant. He realized in the battlefield that God, Almighty Jehovah, does not need five chances. One is enough. In fact, God has already done it; He is just looking for an excuse to accomplish what He has already purposed to do. The stone was that excuse. God sets up. David knew Goliath was walking into a trap. David knew that all battles are first won in the spirit.

Every trained Israelite soldier who was present knew that approaching Goliath was suicide. Others had even developed 'diseases' to excuse themselves from the battle front. The giant's stare melted their spines. They went back home. Terrible perception. When they looked at Goliath, what did they see? They saw their wives widowed and children being taken care of in orphanages somewhere in slums. Your perception heralds your defeat or your dominion. Choose.

Friend, shortly after the encounter, guess what happened. David's brothers were shouting on top of their voices that David was their kid brother. Eliab, his elder brother, was even the first to say, 'I told you he was gonna do it'. But the fella never 'told' anyone anything. In addition, the friends of David's brothers all told their wives and girl friends that David's brothers were their closest friends. The wives and girlfriends boasted that their men were close to David's brothers. Those who seemed to have no 'connection' envied them like hungry hyenas eyeing a carcass surrounded by lions. Every Jim and Jack and Jane wanted the share of the pie now that the 'impossible' had been done. Do not despair; you are the next person the world is about to say 'I told you,' even if they never 'told' anything. Have that divine perspective. Our blessed perspective. Do not give in or give up to evil. God has set you up for victory.

B. ELISHA

> 2 Kings 6:15 *When the servant of the man of God got up early the next morning and went outside, there were troops, horses, and chariots everywhere. "Oh, sir, what will we do now?" the young man cried to Elisha.*
> (NLT)

A glance at the invading army—apache helicopters, tanks, humvees and marines made Elisha's servant perspire a 100 liters of sweat. He just said to his master, 'The end has come. Let us make things right with God for the hour of our death has come. May God receive our souls.' He bowed his head like a wilting flower and made the sign of the cross...

'What's the matter?' Elisha asked.

'The end has come. Come and see.' The servant told him as he led him outside to see the invading army.

'Is that what you called me out to see?' Elisha asked in shock.

'Y-yes,' the servant stuttered.

'Our prisoners?' Elisha enquired.

'W-what?! The the the marine corps, the humvees and apache? Master I understand you are in shock. Even God knows this is beyond Him,' The servant was more sure than ever before that the shock of being surrounded had just given his boss cerebral malaria. *Elisha was hallucinating*. The servant was sure.

Being a prophet and knowing how carnal his servant was, Elisha knew that no sermon could change the man's poor perspective. Therefore, he asked the Lord to open his eyes. **In other words, Elisha asked God to broaden his servant's perception, from the physical into the spiritual.** The servant saw what Elisha had been seeing all that time. When you see what others see in the spirit arguments cease. Limited perspective or perception is the greatest cause of fear and arguments. The spiritually blind make too much noise, because they see little. Their mouths do the compensation. After seeing in the spirit, a smile flashed on Elisha's servant's face and he wiped sweat from his brow that cold morning. He dipped his left hand into his trouser pocket, drew out a piece of paper and tore the Will he had hastily began to compose. Elisha and his servant looked at the same situation, but drew different conclusions. Why? Perception. One saw beyond the ordinary world, the other could not go beyond the optical eyes. Elisha saw in the spirit. He saw victory. The servant only saw the enemy forces. He saw defeat. **What do you see in your situation?** Pastor we are finished. They have taken over. Speak for yourself. As you read you will discover certain things about the devil, that makes him not so great after all. The devil can make 99 moves. God only one. The game is over. Done and dusted. God is never late. Even dead situations He resurrects! Don't fear, have faith in Him, with whom, it is never too late.

1 Samuel 13:11 *And Samuel said, "What have you done?" And Saul said, "When I saw that the people were scattered from me, and that you did not come within the days appointed, and that the Philistines gathered together at Michmash,* 12 *"then I said, 'The Philistines will now come down on me at Gilgal, and I have not made supplication to the LORD.' Therefore I felt compelled, and offered a burnt offering."* 13 *And Samuel said to Saul, "You have done foolishly. You have not kept the Commandment of the LORD your God, which He commanded you. For now the LORD would have established your kingdom over Israel forever.*

(NKJV)

Common sense fails Saul completely. He thinks God is late. He never is. But it does appear so, from our limited perspective, doesn't it? Your formula will land you into deeper problems. His, will not. Humble yourself and follow Him. The world we live in has a spiritual dimension to it. Believe it or not. The worst part is that if you do not believe or if you believe and do nothing about it, you will continue being a victim of the onslaught. Believe God. That is your part. Elisha's servant 'died' before his end because of his perception. Until Elisha prayed for his eyes to be opened, hypertension had become the servant's ally. Could it be that some of the afflictions you are facing are due to your poor perception of life?

Dangerous and deliberate schemes are being manufactured. Today there is a strange perception on miracles among some groups of Christians. Anyone moving in the miraculous is a Satanist. The one who is not is the true child of God. That is inferior Christianity. Inferior perception. The Bible is full of miracles. Yes, it is true the devil performs miracles. Some people who are working miracles are truly children of the devil. And the worst part is, a desperate person makes no distinction between a miracle from God and a miracle from the devil. Beware.

Examining carefully what comes your way is critical. While it is true there are miracle workers who are being used by the devil, realize that someone may just talk you out of your inheritance, the miracles of God. There is a dimension I would like you to understand. A sinister, deliberate scheme to deprive God's children what is rightfully theirs. This plot reduces the supernatural dimension of Christianity to a level where God's children live like orphans. Men and women of God who are true vessels of God are constantly ridiculed. The ministry of the Holy Spirit in their lives is reduced, then sidelined. What happens next Teddy?

Evil spirits unleash oppression. What the devil is trying to do is to deceive you out of your rightful perception to a place where he can constantly oppress you. Do you know that 'oppression' actually means 'fraud?' Fraud is illegal anywhere anytime on earth, be it in the physical or the spiritual. There must be no more fraud in your life!

Get this line carefully. The Spirit of God is just talking to you. **It is not everyone who does not believe in miracles who really does not believe in miracles**. Anne read that again. They are trying to change you. Look at this best kept secret of Satan: **Children of darkness do not change their position, they just change their Opposition!** I commend them for their seriousness. May we take a leaf from the great book they have written. We are not in their league, especially looking at how easily they fool us. Their pretence, that charade

> Children of darkness do not change their position, they just change their Opposition!

they are putting up is taking you away from your ultimate answer. The Gospel is power packed. Miracles must follow. In order for the devil to be effective, he has to know what is true and what is false. That way he can point you nicely in the wrong direction. A deceiver is one who knows what is right from what is wrong. The Gospel is packaged with the miraculous. It is your portion. But the devil does not want you to know this. Do you know that one of the names of Jesus in the Bible is **Miracles?** Expect nothing less.

C. LEPERS

2 Kings 7:1 *Then Elisha said, Hear ye the word of the LORD; Thus saith the LORD, Tomorrow about this time shall a measure of fine flour be sold for a shekel, and two measures of barley for a shekel, in the gate of Samaria.* *2a Then a lord on whose hand the king leaned answered the man of God, and said, Behold, if the LORD would make windows in heaven, might this thing be?*

All I desire is to help you tune your perspective to that which is God's perspective. Faith is doing things from God's perspective all the time. Your perspective is wrong if it does not agree with God's perspective. Let God be true and every man a liar. I choose His perspective. His perspective is my perspective. I refuse to accept what my eyes are telling me or what my ears are whispering to me, even my feelings I put them on the shelf, I choose what He says. His Word is always correct even if what I am seeing is telling me the opposite. John that must be your stance!

But it is here where confusion reigns. Many think God's will or perspective for us is that which is boring, and all the *sweetlings* of life are for the devil and his kids. (*I must have missed the time a Third Testament was made. And who died in that Testament, the devil's uncle?*) It is either God the Father of the Lord Jesus and our Father is good or

He is **bad!** God's children must know His true Character. Jesus, the Bible says, is the express image or true Character of God. You look at Jesus in the Gospels and you will know the nature of God. The Church has even misled the world into believing evil things that happen are from God. When an earthquake or a tsunami damages a place what do you call that? *An act of God.* That is blasphemy. If you want to know acts of God go to the book of **Acts** for a start! On second thought, they could be right. It is an act of God. God HAARP.

1. Social Perspective

Calls to 'hear' the Word of the Lord produced the opposite result in 2 Kings 7. Why is it that instructions are the hardest things to follow? Elisha told the people to **hear**, meaning pay extra attention and obey. But the king's *economic advisor* began to argue. Sometimes you can be too educated and too courageous to your own destruction. You do not boast against God and get away with it. The people here had been crying to God for deliverance. When God answered by the man of God Elisha, they started arguing. So what did they want?

Are you in trouble?

Yes

Do you want deliverance?

Yes

Okay. This is what the Lord is saying.

Uh. No.

No?

No.

Okay wise guy, any bright ideas?

Desperation is in the air in 2 Kings 6: 27. Even the King threw away his royal regalia and put on sackcloth. The *Economic Advisor* cried foul. But listen carefully why this fella argued with God's Word. In 2 Kings 6:25 we see a pint or half a kilo of dove droppings (guano), being sold at US $640. That is the rate of gold! Then Elisha comes and says 8 gallons (about 36 kilos) of flour will cost $128 in 24 hours! That is like saying though today we are buying a barrel of oil at $420, tomorrow all the prices of food will be cut by more than 90%! Bread will not cost $20, but 20 cents! Elisha was saying, 'Your Excellency, ladies and gentlemen, the recession is over.' Just like that? Would you believe or would you believe skeptically? Some Christians are in between. They do not believe God fully. They fear total commitment.

Enraged by the preposterous remarks, the Economic Advisor shook his head and said, 'With all respect Mr. Preacher,' he coughed and adjusted his expensive necktie, 'you can fool this uneducated lot, not me. I don't care which cemetery or seminary you are coming from. This recession can only be overcome when you look at certain policies to reverse the GDP's drop, which is a result of the fall in the index, because according to the Jacobean Principle, the economic exponential rises according to certain fiscal policies, which is, of course a matter of the AD and AS,' he paused for effect, looked at the blank and gaping faces of the disconsolate citizens. He continued, 'I know you don't understand what AD or AS stand for. These things are not taught at seminaries.' He shot Elisha a bitter look and smiled with satisfaction. 'I'm talking about Aggregate Demand and Aggregate Supply.'

Elisha looked at the man and felt sorry. Elisha had been to a place where this fella had never been, and never would—for he died the following day, thanks to his big mouth. (Here is a point to remember about promotion.) Many people want to be promoted. It is good to be promoted. However, you must understand that there are only two reasons God promotes. He promotes so that you carry out His desire or He elevates you so that your destruction is inevitable. We must take seriously the positions we ascend to, there is accountability. Haven't you realised that most people become evil when they occupy positions of power? God knew it, but He had to bring them to a place where they would also bear witness when He judges them, that they are wicked. And His judgement very deserved. What happened to the economic advisor who opposed Elisha? He was elevated to a position where his destruction would be swift. **My prayer is that you are not like him.** When the *Economic Advisor* was opposing Elisha he did not know that Elisha had crossed a river by parting the water. He did not know that Elisha had seen Elijah defy gravity, death and all the laws in between when he ascended into heaven with chariots of fire, without a space suit and the fire never burnt him! NASA has not come close to trying that out, with all the technological advancement. He did not know Elisha operated outside the physical realm. He could blind an army by a faint whisper. He did not know that Elisha had received double portion of anointing from Elijah. He was no ordinary man. **Are you ordinary? God forbid.** You cannot be if you are really born again. It is impossible. Very impossible!

Few believe in such gigantic miracles. Elisha said within 24 hours the economy would change. The Economic Advisor told the people that it would not happen even if God had the desire to do it. That day both Elisha and the Economic Advisor went home thinking the other was foolish. And they all said, 'We shall see'. One thinks the other is a fool and the other returns the compliment. And everyone is happy. The world is wonderful. In our own eyes we are all wise. But the Economic Advisor was ignorant. His perception was narrow. This is the danger of human knowledge. It is limited.

2Corinthians 2:14 *But the natural man does not receive*
the things of the Spirit of God, for they are
foolishness to him; nor can he know
them, because they are

spiritually discerned.
(NKJV)

Human knowledge will limit even what to expect from God. The miracles that your mind can comprehend God can do, but something beyond? No, not even God. Clap for yourself. You are a genius.

Friend, I believe in God who changes things in 24 literal hours. In fact, God can change situations in seconds. Good luck with your god *(Meni)* who has to wait for you for 300 million years to evolve to cure a headache! But you my friend are not experimenting with your life. My Teacher of Biology used to say: Never experiment with your body; you may never live to see the conclusion. Friend, never experiment with life for you may live to see a very hot conclusion—Hell. I thank Jesus for you. You are the kind that does not experiment. Verse two ends tragically as God gives the Economic Advisor the boot for noise making. When someone says 'hear', you hear. 'Hear' does not mean commence debate. Unbelief is a disqualifier. And just as the second verse ended on a sad note, verse three starts on a sad one too. We see four lepers hurdled together. The devil has a way of bringing people together for a pity party. I have seen this often. Small groups of people with 'sores' licking one another and speaking nothings to one another. If you have a situation never go to people who have a similar problem, they will only sympathize. Look for those who will give you a **holy** solution.

Grief is upon the lepers as they think the problem is now compounded. They are lepers (outcasts) and they are starving to death. So a party had to be held. A pity party. In the pity party state, they forgot they were at the **gate**. You are at your gate! Get up. Dust off self–pity. Shake it off in the name of Jesus Christ of Nazareth. The lepers plucked up courage and got up when they realized it was now a matter of life and death. It is true they were lepers, but they were Israelites, Covenant people too. **The covenant outweighs the leprosy. Your situation does not cancel who you are in Christ. It doesn't!** Friend, you are a Christian. What happened in the past happened. Start afresh. Get up. Get up now!

Hours of self–pity proved unfruitful and the lepers decided to **talk life**. Davie, do you know that the wisest people on earth are Christians? I can't believe their supernatural wisdom. Even the devil is in shock. The devil is almost in a comma. Christians will talk from morning to evening about a problem that they are facing. They will complain and complain. But praying they will not. Why can't they realize that prayer is talking and use that moment to talk to Dad? It takes time, a mouth and a listener to complain. You always complain to someone. It takes time, a mouth and God for you to pray. Which one is beneficial? Be your own judge. **Listen dear corporal, only losers complain, champions do not.** God has never known you as a loser. Why are you forcing yourself to be a loser? Begin to talk your success. Begin to speak life upon your life. Perception matters. When you stand up and begin to talk scriptures, you find out that God has already provided for you. There is no opposition. Are you born again? The devil is disarmed. It is important to note that the lepers decided to move at a time which was not favorable. Nightfall. Just when everyone says this situation is beyond God, that is when He likes stepping in. When the sun is setting down on your hope, rest assured He will appear! I know what I am talking about. I have lived it.

Psalm 112:4 *Even in darkness light dawns*
for the upright, for the gracious
and compassionate and
righteous man
(NIV)

2. Scripture Verses Situation

Even when tears are pouring down, total confusion is upon you, life's pressures seem to overwhelm you, follow His promise. There was a time when I was overwhelmed with intense pressure, year in year out and when I saw it was now a life style I asked God, 'Am I in your Will?' And the Lord didn't waste time in responding and it was one question God has answered speedily. He said, 'You are right in the center of my Will.' Listen, my friend. Calm down. Do you need a miracle in your life? Are you really sure you need a miracle? I am sure you don't. Almost everyone is ready to say they need a miracle, but the question of the millennium is:

'Do you really qualify?'

'To receive a miracle you need qualifications?'

'You are correct Tom. Very correct.'

'How can you qualify Pastor?'

'Simple. Let your situation go beyond human capacity then you qualify.'

When the Egyptian army is after you, the desert and mountains on the sides and in front the Red sea, friend you qualify. Rejoice. Like the lepers march on courageously, God has a miracle for you.

> 2 Kings 7:6 *for the Lord had caused the Arameans to hear the sound of chariots and horses and a great army, so that they said to one another, "Look, the king of Israel has hired the Hittite and Egyptian kings to attack us!" 7 So they got up and fled in the dusk and abandoned their tents and their horses and donkeys. They left the camp as it was and ran for their lives.*
> (NIV)

The devil like the Arameans is on the run. He is all the time fleeing from God's Word, which is the sword of the Spirit. The lepers got up and entered the city. Enter your city. It is God's desire for you.

Ecclesiastes 10:15 *The labour of the foolish wearieth every one of them, because he knoweth not how to go to the city.*

I am convinced you are not foolish. You know how to get to your city. Amen. 'The City' here does not mean Paris, New York, Lusaka or Tokyo. It means a better life. Do you know how to have better life? Come to Jesus. The goodness of God is unending. Prophet Elisha delivered God's Word. The instrument of implementation was **anyone**. The king and his people could not take a step to receive the miracle. Instead, they found it a joy in making stew out of their babies. (We are doing the same with 'cloned' fetuses today) Even the king parading himself in sackcloth was nothing. When God told him to take a step, he clung to his bed like a leech on human skin! He was full of fear. Read 2 Kings 6. *What do you see?* Fear.

III. MAIN HINDRANCE

A. Secret of Fear

✓ As long as fear is ruling in your life nothing will be done. Fear immobilizes. Fear is very destructive. People make wrong decisions because of fear. Good people do bad things because of fear. Bad people do bad things because of fear.

✓ But fear is not the problem. **Fear is a child of false knowledge or wrong perception.** Perception is the main problem. You may quote scriptures nicely, but your understanding is the issue. Do you really understand? What is your perception of that scripture? **Fear comes from wrong knowledge—which is really ignorance, all the time**. The devil only attacks people with the idea

49

that *maybe this person is ignorant of this*...did you know that? Don't forget this secret. When the devil attacks he is not sure! Always. When fear comes to you next time just ask yourself what you don't know about that situation. Tell yourself, 'What is it that I must know to end this?' As the Holy Spirit begins to lead you the fear starts evaporating. Interesting. Fear is simply capitalizing on your ignorance, on what you don't know. With this tip, you will be courageous and the devil will have a hard time facing you. Because you know. The devil runs his kingdom on fear and deception. Deception so that people do not really know the real thing. Because if they do they will say to him, 'Alas, we thought you were something, but you are not.'

Clap for yourself, you have just graduated. God has declared He is doing great and mighty things in these last days. Has He picked the vessels?

It is an open cheque. Sign in your name. God is changing *the economies* and guess who He is going to use? Correct. The lepers! The nobodies. The down trodden. The unknown. You.

Jesus made it clear that God delights in answering our prayers, so that our joy is full. Meaning? You can't have full joy without answered prayer. Unfortunately, God does not answer many people's prayers because they are not expecting Him to. When the Apostle Peter was in prison a group of prayer warriors stood together and prayed for his release. When God responded, they said, 'Impossible'. *Why were they praying in the first place?* Poor perspective.

You believe God uses people?

Yes.

So, He has chosen you

Me? Impossible.

Knowledge is important to avoid unnecessary slip-ups. I remember a discussion we had with some dear saints. One sister could not be swayed from her stance that God has predestined some people to go to hell, no matter what they do. She believed God wants some people to go and suffer in Hell. Just there I said, 'Let's keep quiet. The Holy Spirit is telling me something.' Everyone kept quiet. Then I said, 'The Lord is just telling me that you are one of those He has predestined to go to hell.' You should have seen her reaction and the way others laughed at her. She said it in all colors that it was impossible. Her place is in Heaven with Jesus. Then I told the dear saint this, 'Why are you comfortable if it is someone else not you?' Friend, if someone tells you some people are predestined to go to Hell, he or she is the one, not you. If someone says the Word of God I'm sharing with you does not work, do not argue. For them it does not, but for you it does. Perspective is everything.

Looking at life, I see many who sincerely believe God is supernatural. When they turn the pages of the Bible, every scripture exudes the supernatural, the miraculous. But these dear saints shut down literally. They fear if they believe in miracles they are going to be deceived. **What they do not know is that the fear to be deceived could itself be deception.** You are dealing with a cunning devil who wants you leading a natural life instead of a supernatural one. Why? He has many reasons for doing that. And as you read on you will understand why. The Gospel is supernatural. It comes packaged with miracles. You don't go looking for them; the preaching itself has enough power to demolish opposition. I have seen souls being saved from committing suicide by the preaching of the word alone. Fifteen precious lives so far have been saved, not by any special revelation, but by mere preaching and burdens of suicide destroyed. That is why the men and women of God should preach His Word and not theirs because some people you meet today you may never meet again. They will be killed by the devil. The responsibility may just fall on us in the pulpits. Let us have the right perspective in all we do and we will shine brighter. The devil does not want you with a proper perspective, because something happened and I would like you to know what it is. Here is how it all started a long time ago and the reasons he distorts people's perspectives...

2.

KING OF REBELLION: LUCIFER

Isaiah 14:12 *How art thou fallen from*
heaven, O Lucifer, son of
the morning!

AFTER the fall, Lucifer which means Day Star or Morning Star became Satan (Adversary, Accuser). It is important to note that he was not the only star. Angels (*and now even the righteous people*) are called stars. But that Lucifer was a notch above the masses is without any doubt, crystal clear from the scriptures. He was an exalted cherub—one of a special kind of angels that cover God's Throne. He was extremely beautiful, covered with all kinds of precious stones Ezekiel 28:13. Heads of angels turned as he toddled majestically on the beautiful boulevards of Heaven. God was happy with him. God loved him. But all the attention he got, seemed to have gotten to his mind. His good looks corrupted him. He forgot the source of the gift. Do not magnify the gift more than the Giver.

Ezekiel 28:17 *Thine heart was lifted up because of thy beauty, thou hast corrupted*
thy wisdom by reason of thy brightness: I will
cast thee to the ground, I will lay thee
before kings, that they may
behold thee

I.   HIS THIRST FOR POWER

Because of the beauty and splendor, this anointed and covering cherub corrupted his wisdom and began to seek power! **He wanted to rule. He refused anything or anyone to stand between him and his goal, power.** With the anointed cherub commanding music, he became big headed. This king of rebellion led an army to oust Jehovah out of power.

Isaiah 14:11 *All your pomp has been brought down to the grave,*
along with the noise of your harps; maggots are
spread out beneath you and worms
cover you. (Emphasis added)

And because everyone acknowledged his gift, he found a perfect story for a good following. **Do not use your gift for selfish gain. Use it in humility to bless the one who gave it to you.** The devil used his gift and influence to pull to himself a third of a humanly uncountable number of angels.

Revelation 12:4 *His tail swept a third of the*
stars out of the sky and flung
them to the earth
(NIV)

The God of the Bible is God of holiness, He dwells not with sin. Musician or not, cherub or not you go down. God stripped Lucifer of his beauty and his dream of power faded. Ezekiel 28:16. Satan looking at him today is not so appealing, but he disguises himself at times for the sake of keeping up appearances as some beautiful being. 2 Corinthians 11:14. The truth is, Satan is ugly and his bunch of deputies—the demons are. (*In 1998, some people thought I had gone overboard when I mentioned that demons have a terrible stench. I'm glad many are confirming it. Demons stink. This is not to speak insultingly but it is the truth as things really are.*) Satan at one time had the idea that maybe God was afraid of competition. Well he just discovered the opposite. God refused to kill or destroy Satan immediately.

Most dictators are super cowards. They cover up their fear with force

God the Father of our Lord Jesus is not a despot. Instant anger or reaction to an accusation or challenge is a sign of weakness. All despots fear to be challenged. Did you know that? They fear to be challenged because they know deep down in their hearts, there is someone better than they are. Most dictators are super cowards. They cover up their fear with force. Ask pharaoh, how he feared the Hebrew baby boys, ask Herod how he went into spasms when he heard another king was born. These despots all tried to destroy their opposition in infancy. Ivy, do you know that somebody somewhere shudders by the simple mention of your name?

'Pastor Keyworth, are you talking to me?'

'No Ivy, am talking to your auntie.'

But do you know where this inferiority complex is coming from? The devil. It's the way he feels about you. He wants you destroyed before you know very much. Once you are mature he can't handle you. But God our Father is different. He doesn't fear anything or anyone. Talk about freedom of speech, expression, press freedom. Isn't it funny that others can speak, but you can't speak? Look at our sweet system of democracy. It says there must be freedom of speech and expression. Christians with eyes popping out of their sockets like pop corns, can't believe their luck. Freedom of speech and expression? The Christian starts preaching against prostitution, witchcraft, homosexuality and Satanism. Then the system closes on them. They are infringing on other people's rights. The Christian's rights don't matter. To their shock, the deflated Christian now realizes, the freedom of speech and expression is for others not him. 'But... but I...I believe in demo...' he stammers. The real fangs and claws of democracy have just been bared. Ready to strike. Democracy. Democracy. Now we know we are not of this world. It is just bad that we are learning it the hard way. The world believes in gagging the one who wants to speak, but God is different. God has let Satan roam so he could prove his case. God simply said if you are as great as you claim to be, prove yourself before the universe. Prove it that IAM is bad. Satan realized his folly a long time ago. Man has not. Unfortunately.

Cast down, embarrassed and bitter, Satan realized his time was up. He began another campaign. Satan has tried to win man on his side. He wants people to think God is a dictator who is scared that man will discover how to be great, just as God is. Satan tried to convince Adam to do this foolish thing. Thank God for Adam he could not be fooled by the devil. Adam's folly though, nearly gave the devil a heart attack. He convulsed. **Adam was not deceived by the devil, but he still swallowed the fruit!**

> 1 Timothy 2:14 *And it was not Adam who was deceived by Satan. The woman was deceived, and sin was the result.*

Up to now the devil can't understand it. I can't either.

Deception has become Satan's way of life. Whenever he speaks sincerely, he is lying. He has been lying about a lot of things in your life. **All his lies are being exposed and the more you see it the more you should take your position.** The devil will fail to deceive you now. By deception he craftily got the authority from Adam and became the ruler of the world. (It's good to be mindful of the advice you receive. Someone could just be eyeing your position.) Adam had not seen it coming. Satan being a great tactician made sure he attacked Adam before he ever had any child. Whatever Adam would produce after the fall was going to be corrupt. From God's standard humanity or the human race was doomed from the very beginning. Satan simpered. He had just checkmated God. All Heaven was shell-shocked. All the angels froze in the midst of their halleluiahs. They all looked to God. Perspiring.

II. HIS TERRIBLE MISJUDGMENT

Do not despair. Satan has one settled issue. He cannot fight God. **God is Inviolate**. That is one attribute, which has not been emphasized. We have mentioned omniscience, omnipotence and others, but this one we have thrown away. The battle between God and Satan was settled once and for all. God cannot fight Satan one on one. That would be abuse of office by God. You do not need hydrogen bombs, stealth bombers, jaguars, F-series jets to attack a fly. It is a total waste of power. A fly by nature has a limited life span to start with. Simply use a swat to deal with the nuisance. The devil was judged. To arrest him it will not take God coming down, but one lone angel with heavenly handcuffs. He will not even drop a rivulet of sweat when doing it!

> Revelation 20:1 *And I saw an angel come down from heaven,*
> *having the key of the bottomless pit and a great chain*
> *in his hand.² And he laid hold on the dragon,*
> *that old serpent, which is the Devil,*
> *and Satan, and bound him*
> *a thousand years*

It is that easy with God. The big devil the world shudders before will be arrested by one Angel Police *(it should have been by the Zambia Police)*. Understand who God is first. **God is Inviolate—meaning you can neither attack Him nor harm Him.**

And how can you kill what cannot be killed? You need infinite miracles to do that. That is the first thing Satan discovered. And he rested his case in shame. The apostle Paul, during his crazy days was given the same message in Acts 9:5. You try to slap God you find yourself harmed. Jesus was saying you cannot lift your bare foot and stamp on a sharp iron nail. It is one sure way of calling the paramedics! And the paramedics are not coming to help the nail.

God is Inviolate—meaning you can neither attack Him nor harm Him.

> Joel 3:4b *"…Are you repaying me for something I have*

done? If you are paying me back, I will
swiftly and speedily return on your
own heads what you
have done."
(NIV)

Enveloped in the revelations of God the Apostle Paul learnt that God is not simple. You do not play games with God Almighty and come out on top. In 1 Timothy 6:16 he learns by the Holy Spirit that if to start with you cannot approach God how can you attack Him? The unapproachable light mentioned refers both to God's purity—which no sinner can find peace in and it refers to God's intense Power or Presence. Before reaching the sun, you would sublime or vaporize a million times over. The sun as we know it is unapproachable. The energy coming from the sun to the earth is almost negligible if quantified, in comparison to its total output. But that negligible energy keeps us panting for icebergs! This makes one realize God the creator of such a thing is not a joke. Approaching the sun can't be tried even in one's imagination! **Your brains will sublime!!**

Revelation 4:5 *From the throne came flashes of lightning,*
rumblings and peals of thunder. Before the
throne, seven lamps were blazing.
These are the seven
Spirits of God.
(NIV)

This shows us the strange angle of God. Lightning and thunder are the norm in God's presence. Lightning is high voltage—we are talking about thousands of degrees in Celsius. About 30 000°C. Between you and me we know, what we are given is the tip of a giant iceberg. God is a consuming fire, Hebrews 12:29. He is hotter than this simple light we call the sun! You think demons fear Him for nothing? You must be kidding. They know better.

Ever seen kids playing the game of Barricade? The strong ones hold hands (*clasping hands at the elbows*) and they dare their friend to come and pass. If he fails to break the hold another takes his position. God likes that game. He has not just found willing players. He says 'If you dare put your strongest barricade, during my evening walk, without any sweat I will wipe out everything by my presence!' Isaiah 27:4. That settled, Satan could not fight Him, common sense, but he embarked on psychological warfare. He gets God's new friend—humans, and torments God. And he said, 'I got you!' Satan skipped and hopped. God looked at him and smiled. Satan froze. All angels in heaven gathered.

'Gaby, come and see this. He's smiling.'

'What's He going to do?'

'I have not, the faintest idea'

'Mike we are really in for a treat. Keep your eyes open.'

'I ain't even blinking son, not today'

And so went the conversation between Angel Gabriel and Arch Angel Michael. God didn't take it lying down. He was thinking, then He responded. God made a move. More than any chess grand master could. A move that the words **Super Genius** are a terrible misnomer to use in describing Him. They fail to describe a trillionth of who He really is....

3.

SATAN SEES RED

Matthew 1:1 *A record of the genealogy*
of Jesus Christ the son
of David

Isaiah 53:2 *He grew up before him like a tender shoot, and like a*
root out of dry ground. He had no beauty or majesty
to attract us to him, nothing in his
appearance that we should
desire him

(NIV)

ALL the Adamic race was doomed when Adam and Eve fell. Despite having lost the splendor of Heaven, Satan consoled himself with this prize—power. The nations were in his hands, Luke 4:5, 6. God was well checkmated. No wonder heaven was quiet. One could hear a pin drop. But God had to respond in a very unique way—in wisdom. This was the beginning of the greatest display of wisdoms between God and Satan. God's move was with a pawn, Jesus.

But, as you can see from the scriptures, Jesus did not have that imposing presence so the devil chuckled. He underrated our Savior. Jesus, a simple looking pawn, a David coming to meet Goliath, came to face Satan one on one for the freedom of humans. Satan laughed and just said, *'Are you sure you are Wisdom? Is this your best move?'* Satan is Pride. Note that I didn't write 'proud' but 'pride'. At this point or stage, it is important to note that there had not been any replacement for the disgraced Lucifer. No wonder he was still revered and he felt invincible. This tickled his ego. Nothing could make him boast like knowing there was no replacement. In the Book of Job, the Bible mentions Satan in heaven. He knew there was no replacement. He felt special. Very special.

Calm and focused, Jesus surprised everyone. After 30 years of silence, He began His ministry. He loosed prison doors. The sick, maimed, demon possessed, the dead... the list is as short as eternity, all received His help. A champion had stepped in the ring. Demons complained to Satan that some 'Guy' had forced them out of the houses they had been occupying. They appealed to Satan to address the situation which was now 'unbecoming'. This was the second time angels stopped in the midst of their halleluiahs. Satan had no choice. Satan had to dig into his arsenal and come up with the winning formula. The calm young man, Jesus, was no longer calm. He had to be dealt with. Satan reached for death and unleashed it. He killed Jesus. What he never understood was that in God the Father's Wisdom, Jesus had taken on the nature of Adam.

Hebrews 2:14 *Since the children have flesh and blood, he too shared in their humanity so that by his death he might destroy him who holds the power of death—that is, the devil—¹⁵ and free those who all their lives were held in slavery by their fear of death. ¹⁶ For surely it is not angels he helps, but Abraham's descendants.*

(NIV)

I. HE KILLS JESUS

Jesus actually brought death to the Adamic nature. He died with it. *'He has killed them! The hero has just killed what he came to save!'* The devil laughed his lungs out. The angels scratched their heads in confusion. Satan's strength was death. And he unleashed it. Man's only hope, Jesus was dead. The angels looked to God again. God just pointed to the earth. Their gazes followed the direction of His finger. Satan nailed Jesus to his torture rack—the cross, the most vicious form of torture known to mankind, he said to Jesus, *'That should teach you a lesson, not to come here and play hero with me'.*

Demons danced around and held a get–together. Glasses were heard clicking. Chickens and turkeys squawked for the last time under the heavy hilarity. Seven course meals were being served. They all had just heard Jesus surrender or give up when He said, *'It is finished.'* There was shouting. Heavy metal rock was blaring from the dark pit of hell. But the devils had heard wrongly. **What was finished was the devil's dominion over man.** In the midst of their party in Hell, the doors opened, guards flew in, crushing to the floor, and smashing some tables in the process. Jesus, the new invincible man, with a smile on his face, stood leaning against the door, rubbing His knuckles and looking at Satan. 'Impossible!' Satan yelled. 'Guards seize Him'. The deputies tried to stop Jesus. He slapped them until they all fled changing their addresses. Others peeped from a distance as Jesus dragged Satan out amidst Satan's *'I'm sorry I really didn't mean it. Please don't do this. I swear I'm sorry. I know I'm The Liar but I mean it this time. Master I'm sorry'.*

Every person must hear the greatest humiliation story ever told. The Bible says Jesus appeared so that He might 'Destroy' the devil. The word for destroy means

✓ to make useless

✓ to render ineffective

A few questions arise from there. If Jesus has rendered the devil of no use, why are you making him useful by reaching out for his solutions? If you really hate the devil as a Christian, then you must hate even the 'chocolates' he dishes out. Is the devil effecting or exerting his influence in your life? It is impossible. It is not supposed to happen.

Fortunately, for the devil, only a few people understand the full implications when the Bible says the devil moves around like a roaring lion looking for someone to devour in 1 Peter 5:8. That tells me that the devil does not attack anyhow. Get this, your life depends on it. **The devil looks for the ignorant, the immature, the unsuspecting and pounces on them. Why? He**

has no power. He is weak. He depends on tricks, tricking the ignorant. This is why you must not leave your life to chance. Be informed. **Tricking the world into evil is the devil's greatest agenda.** Many people have unfortunately, succumbed to this folly. The roaring lion it must be understood, also transforms himself into a harmless looking angel. We have seen examples of some of our celebrities. They have to pay back for their popularity with pornography. We call them 'porn stars'. Hmm. Somebody must redefine 'star'. How do you combine porn and star? And these stars we hail, shape our lives. We are now close buddies. We even give them the pulpit of Jesus. They preach their gospel, from Jesus' pulpit. *We are sick!* We literally drool for them. We are panting to be like them.

Good Lord! Though wicked most of them are, we grovel, even leaving our Bibles behind to lick their feet. After all, we believe in feet washing. We take their songs, where the songs mention 'together' we qualify this as Christian songs. *A stupid army!* Their standard becomes our standard. Do we know what is going on? The master puppeteer who knows that sometimes 'gentleness' appeals to the flesh, is at the end of the tether, pulling us into his fold. Compromise is a big tool in Satan's claws. Let's have a stance as God's children. The devil will use even that which is appealing to us. Be alert. But we know this for sure, whether he transforms himself and threatens, he is still the same useless ineffective devil. **The mask he puts on does not change his position. He is defeated. This must reflect in our lives!** The devil is a pretender. By pretending to be what he is not, he is oppressing some ignorant people. If the devil comes to me and tells me to lay my machine gun down, and the devil lays down his gun first, only one of us has lost. And that's me. For with a certainty the devil is disarmed. If he is, then the thing he just laid down is a toy from China, it is not a real gun. Don't you ever settle for compromise!

Grant, there is only one way of knowing the devil is not armed, by resisting him. All he can shoot are flares. Darts. In 1 Peter 5:9 the Bible tells us to put our foot down! When the devil realizes you know, he flees. **Authority over the devil and his**

kingdom is for all Christians. It is important to know what the Spirit has set forth as special ministries and what is for every believer. The truth is, Jesus is Lord and the entire universe does not question it. Jesus has given every believer authority over the devil. The devil is not supposed to be busy in your life. The devil as a roaring lion, will use fear to scare you. He wants you to feel insecure in Christ. But you must understand that you are hidden in Christ. Don't let the devil's roar scare you out of your hidden position. When you feel very unsafe in Christ, you try your own means. You come out and try to out sprint the lion. Your idea, you realise, is the shortest route to hell. Get this, for Satan does not want you to know it.

Hell does not want you to know what really happened that day. **Before you ever bowed to Jesus, Satan did. This is not a joke! Before you ever confessed that Jesus is Lord, Satan did.** Do not let his roar fool you. When Jesus whacked the devil in the greatest show down, He posed a question. *'Who is in charge?'* Satan, trembling and on his knees, looked around and said in a shaky voice, *'Is there anyone apart from you my Lord?'* That is the basis for Jesus saying in

> Matthew 28:18b *…All power is given*
> *unto me in heaven and*
> *in earth.*

There was no one to challenge Jesus anymore. He got the crown of Master of the universe. The pawn had now become King. Please do not lose me here. Jesus defeated Satan as a sinless human being. That is why

> Hebrews 10:5 *Therefore, when Christ came into*
> *the world, he said: "Sacrifice and*
> *offering you did not desire,*
> *but a body you prepared*
> *for me.* (NIV)

A body have you prepared for me. Do you have a body? It was prepared for you to do good for God your Dad. Do not misuse it. The Owner has the final say over it. That is borrowed property. You are just a steward, a caretaker.

In God's Wisdom, Satan could have tried to get away with the destruction of the first Adam, but not Jesus the second Adam. God was determined to give him the shocker of his miserable remaining days. What Satan had not known was that God never gives up on people, people give up on Him! God had not given up on Adam. Jesus was another Adam.

> 1 Corinthians 15:45 *So it is written: "The first man Adam became a living being"* ⁴⁷ *; the last Adam, a life-giving spirit*
> (NIV)

God was saying you might have destroyed the first Adam, but not the second. In fact, I will do you a favor. I'll help you destroy the first Adam completely. *Here is where you slow down.* God helped Satan destroy the first Adam. When Jesus went to the cross He was not alone, He carried with Him the old Adamic nature, which was slave to Satan. Satan did not know that. This is one secret Satan wants kept hidden. **When Satan killed Jesus he literally killed what he had control over...the entire sin laden Adamic race.**

The devil took himself out of business. In English, he shot himself in the foot. No, not in the foot. In the head! He committed suicide.

Genesis 3:15 *And I will put enmity between you and the woman, and between your offspring [14] and hers; he will crush [15] your head, and you will strike his heel."*

(NIV)

The old self, the old nature was crucified and do you know why God let it be crucified?

Romans 6:6 *For we know that our old self was crucified with him so that the body of sin might be done away with, that we should no longer be slaves to sin*

When Satan put the last nail in Jesus, he put the last nail in his reign over man. After the Fall, Satan had power and control over the first Adamic nature. But when he killed Jesus, he did not know that he was killing the same **entire Adamic nature he had control over**.

1Corinthians 2:7 *But we speak the wisdom of God in a mystery, the hidden wisdom which God ordained before the ages for our glory,[8] which none of the rulers of this age knew; for had they known, they would not have crucified the Lord of glory.*

(NKJV)

He killed what he had control over—all his subjects. The power that Satan had, the consolation prize he had craftily secured for himself in the Garden of Eden, he had lost clearly on Golgotha and he could do nothing about it. That body he controlled had perished at his own hands. There is nothing as painful as being beaten at your own game and by your own doing. God catches the crafty in their craftiness. 1 Corinthians 3:19. Satan knows that verse more than any person will ever know it.

But the devil does not want you to know that he has no control over you. The new creation is not controlled by the devil; it is led by the Holy Spirit. He guards this secret jealously. Some Christians are wallowing in condemnation because they do not know who they are or what has happened.

The new creation is not controlled by the devil; it is led by the Holy Spirit

In their eyes they see that they are imperfect and it is useless to resist, why not just fall into the cauldron of wickedness? After all, if you can't beat them, join them. The devil is the one who can't beat you. The worst news for him, he can't join you either. Never be fooled by what is happening around us. Those who love the devil, should continue. But you are not like that. You are different. Even if the entire world gangs up against you, the way they did to Jesus, maintain. Soon, it will be over. And you will stand on the podium. Victorious. Satan seems to be 99% in control of the physical world. Many people see Satan in control. There are some of us, who see in the spirit. We know better. Nothing. Nothing. Nothing will fool me. I know. The devil is very defeated.

II. HE LOSES EVERYTHING

Jesus, by His death on the cross has outlawed the first Adamic nature. It is the only thing that Satan can rule over. It is important to understand this truth. The first Adamic nature was taken from the shelves of the world super markets about 2000+ years ago. Why? That was its sell by date. Continuing to live in that outlawed nature is very disastrous to your health. It is not Y2K compliant! It will crash. A person who is not born again is

2000+ years outdated. And that's not a joke. Friend that kind of life you are leading isn't cool. That's not in vogue. Come here we show you the in-thing. You want the latest fashion? This is the place.

Knowing this will save many Christians heartaches. There are two races here. The old and the new. You cannot explain it all to the old race, they will not get it. They cannot grasp why you are different and the result? Attacking you. Some people who attack Christians do not even listen to what they are saying. I remember in a public place, one man said, 'Christians are weak. That is why Jesus told them to turn the other cheek. And look at the Christian men, they fear girls. That is being weak'. They laughed. I could not resist that kind of temptation. I chipped into their conversation.

I said, 'Which one is easier, to retaliate when someone slaps you or to hold your peace, think about it?'

'I think to retaliate is much easier,' one of the friends responded.

'Good. So are you saying losing temper easily is for the weak?'

'Y-yes,' the second friend responded thoughtfully.

'Good. Now which one is easier, to sleep with someone in an environment that is tantalizing or to refrain? We take it there is no threat of any kind, all things okay.'
They chuckled a bit.

'That is meat. Dead meat,' the first man said.

'So you agree with me that it is harder to keep the zipper up. Because coming down you don't need help, the force of gravity will do the job, right? Friend, then Christians are strong. It is the other way round. Come and join the strong,' I ended.

Keeping your temper under lock and key takes discipline. See? Even a fool knows you do not have to be a genius to lose your temper. You simply throw it on the rubbish heap and it will take you months to find it. Unless one is born-again it is impossible to fully understand who a Christians is. Next time somebody attacks you for being a Christian be aware there are two races. Do not apologize. Apologizing for being a Christian is treason in God's Kingdom. When Jesus got the power and authority what next? **Not only did He get the power He got the name Day Star, Morning Star.** Do you know of a name that means Day Star or Morning Star? Lucifer. Jesus became the Shining star!

Revelation 22:16 *"I, Jesus, have sent my angel to give you²⁸ this testimony for the churches. I am the Root and the Offspring of David, and the bright Morning Star."* (NIV).

Looking at the above scripture critically, we realize this is Satan's second grand possession that just slipped through his wicked tentacles. **God gave out the two things that Satan greatly coveted—Power and name of Morning star.** Halleluiah!! Lucifer is not a bad name. It is a title. A title that many in the dark world have used to worship a fallen creature who once occupied that position. **There is no light in Satan. He is total darkness personified.** There is no illumination from the devil. None. But as the father of lies the devil is a good story teller. He tells them how powerful and how much light he gives or illuminates. What light? Mass murder of other people groups through fabricated diseases? Mass murder of lives through concocted economic woes? Mass deception of people in churches, where they think they are serving God, when it is devil worship they are participating in? Jesus, the Son of the true and Living God, Jehovah is the only true light. He is the Bright Morning Star. Wow! But wait. The story does not end there. Satan's best-kept secrets have just been scratched. As Christians, we are jumping with joy and it's biblical. When the wicked are out of power there are shouts of joy! People rejoice when tyrants are killed. Tyrannicide is great news. Understand why we shout. The dictator is out of power. Praise the Lord!!! Praise God for His great works. His wonderful ways. His incomprehensible wisdom. Wow.

Majestically and triumphantly Jesus today is seated on the Right Hand of the Father. Jesus is 100% God and 100% man. As God He needs none to exalt Him, but as an obedient man God has honored his faithfulness and obedience by sitting Him on the Right Hand of God. This is the highest honor that could be given, not to man only but to any being! I know you missed that deliberately. Read it again. What a mystery God's wisdom is. There are great reasons for Jesus being as He is—100% God and 100% man. But it is beyond the scope of this teaching.

Now, as far as God and Satan are concerned your old self—that Adamic nature which housed sin is dead. Do you know that? Most Christians believe they are still from the old Adam. That's why the devil torments them perpetually. **Most Christians are under the impression the devil is in control. He can never be. He also wishes he was in control, but he is not.** Jesus has totally obliterated the enemy. *But Pastor Keyworth, I see the enemy still blazing forcefully.* What do you believe in, God's report or the sense knowledge before you? You must live by faith. If you are not of the first Adam indeed. Understand why it seems the devil is still blazing with force even though Jesus has defeated him.

> Judges 3:1 *These are the nations the LORD left to test all those Israelites who had not experienced any of the wars in Canaan ² (he did this only to teach warfare to the descendants of the Israelites who had not had previous battle experience)…*
> (NIV)

Our God is a wise God. We would not know what it means **to strive against** sin unless the Lord *left nations* to *test* us who have had no experience of what Jesus went through. Now we have battle experience. You are not RE-*defeating* the devil, he is already defeated. **But God wants you to understand the kind of intensity Jesus had to go through to deliver you from the shackles of death!** God wants you to test the battle. This is the wisdom behind Jesus going back to the Father for a little time. When He returns, it is all over. Without this test, many would take lightly their salvation.

Philippians 2:12 *Wherefore, my beloved, as ye have always obeyed, not as in my presence only, but now much more in my absence, work out your own salvation with fear and trembling.*

Only someone who has understood the intensity found in resisting the evil one will acknowledge the need to **'work out your own salvation with fear and trembling.'** When you realize hell is real and the majority are going there, friend you will know how important it is to **work out your own salvation with fear and trembling.** Hell is real, but the devil has thrown in some false notions that hell is just a figment of some deranged Christian's overworking imagination. Why? He wants you to be careless with your life. He wants you to lead life like an animal. I will share, briefly, my personal experience of hell 1995–1996. I went through a concrete tunnel. God showed me what happens when people who are not believers die. Demons come to claim their souls. They literally come to lay hold of the victim. Then two things strike the person.

- ✓ The fear of having missed the Lord Jehovah forever. This is unbearable!

- ✓ The stench—no human on earth today can stand that stench without literally dying.

And this is before you experience the actual fire! Since that period I've had about seven more Hell experiences and about five face to face encounters with Satan. He is real. He is simple looking (though he changes form), but in his face is something I gave him respect for. And that is the ONLY thing I respect about the devil. **Intense determination!** I was shown three sections of Hell. **There are no words to describe hell. NONE!** Let me not get into details. This is my experience, you can believe it or reject it. God doesn't hold you accountable on that. But on the reality of hell, the Bible is clear. It is real. Blessed be our God who is above all wisdom, for he alone is Wisdom. We do not fight as the old Adam, for the old Adam can never stand in the devil's presence and prevail. The old Adam is under the devil. But the second Adam has dominion in His laps. You are of the second Adam. The first is completely gone. Do not be ignorant. Faith is your life. Faith is your key in the second Adam. You are not simple and you cannot be defeated. That, the devil knows very well. Friend, understand who you are and send the devil packing in the next chapter.

4.

ERA OF SAINTS

2 Corinthians 5:17 *Therefore if any man be in Christ,*
he is a new creature: old things are
passed away; behold, all
things are become
new.

A serious comprehension of this scripture is the greatest difference between Satan, who has forged documents, being your master or your slave. When you are born again two things happen to you.

- ✓ **You are a completely new creation.**

- ✓ **And you are in a new world.**

The Bible in Basic English says you are **in a new world**. What is being put across in this book is understanding your life in that new world. **You are in another world.** Not only that, you are not the same. When humanity was destroyed by Satan's move, God started afresh. There was a new beginning. If you are in Christ you are a new creation. Are you in Christ? Are you sure? Many Christians do not know that there have been two creations.

- ✓ **The first creation: First Adam, Genesis to Malachi**

- ✓ **The second creation: Second Adam, Matthew to Revelation**

Moses, you belong to the latter. Listen. Satan's remaining strategy is to question your identity. '**If**' is the word to ponder on in 2 Corinthians 5:17. And the enemy will also question you. It's what he does best. But he is not to blame entirely. Many people do not know who they are. If someone asked me who I am, I speak plainly. I will not say, 'Uh ..um...er...maybe ..' No. I will simply say, 'I'm Keyworth '.

But why hesitating? Don't you know your name or are you afraid of it? The only time I have seen people hesitating to give their names is on roadblocks. There is something wrong with their documents or identity. Spiritual roadblocks are the same. Are you facing a situation that is making you doubt your identity?

I. IDENTITY CHECK

Christ faced the same identity issue in

> Luke 4:3 *And the devil said unto him, If thou be the Son of God, command this stone that it be made bread..*

This verse could be looked at from two angles depending on the interpretation of that little word 'if'. You could take 'if' as it is or read it as 'since.' Here, we take 'if' to mean 'if'. **Your identity is at stake**. You are God's child don't ever doubt it. You must be sure of what you know. Those who are in Christ know it and do not doubt it. Jesus when asked to prove his identity never even bothered. He was too sure to even mention it. Satan is the first witness that this is the Child of God.

Determine that nothing will ever make you doubt that you are a new creation. A child of God. This is something God has never said to any other creation. All the old things are gone. All things have become new. Your inner man is totally new. You have a new mind, the mind of Christ. And your body? It may look the same but you are not the same. That body has a miracle living in it. The Lord Jesus.

Examining Romans 6:6 we see that God did not make you out of the old man. The old man is **d-e-a-d!**

> Romans 6:6 *Knowing this, that our old man is crucified with him, that the body of sin might be destroyed, that henceforth We should not serve sin.*

He **created** you. To create is to produce something out of nothing. If you accept Jesus today, Satan cannot remind you of what happened yesterday. Why? Because you were not yet born! You must be mad to remember. You are a baby. **A newborn baby**.

> 1 Peter 2:2 *As newborn babes, desire the sincere milk of the word, that ye may grow thereby...*

A baby that is born today cannot start remembering what it did yesterday. Stop moving with the baggage of the dead! The old self is dead. The scripture says **knowing this**, that the old man is crucified. Do you **know this**? Stop remembering the dead, the old self and bringing it up. That is necromancy!

Friend, this sounds like a joke, but many have been craftily locked up in the past and the result is that they have no future. Stop meditating on the past, but on the Word of God. Many believe God is judging them for their past sins. Until the time when they have finished 'paying' for their sins they remain trapped. But what sins are you paying for and to whom, dear saint? God does not even know what you are talking about. This is why it is important to understand what has happened to you. **The first Adam never lived by faith that's why he fell. He lived in doubt. God wants those of the second Adam to live by faith.** The life of God is the life of faith.

✓ **Without faith, you are a candidate of hell.**

- ✓ **Without faith, hell will be your life style.**

- ✓ **Without faith you will think life is not fair.**

- ✓ **Without faith you will be bitter.**

- ✓ **Without faith you will go through life believing you are paying for your sins to some cruel god.**

Our Father is not like that. Jesus paid for your sins. His will is for you to live life to the full. So let us ask Him.

'Dad, my friend here would like to know what your **Will is** about this condition, what do you say?'

> Isaiah 43:25 *"I, even I, am he who blots out your transgressions,*
> *__for my own sake, and remembers your sins no more.__ [18]*
> *__"forget the former things; do not dwell on the past.__*
> *[19] See, I am doing a new thing! Now it springs up;*
> *do you not perceive it? I am making a*
> *way in the desert and streams*
> *in the wasteland.*
> (Emphasis added)

Friend God has spoken. See Philippians 3:13. Do you know that it takes rebellion to keep moving in guilt? Yes, you are rebelling against His Word: **Do not dwell on the past!** Forget the former things, why? There is no guilt or condemnation to the one who is in Christ.

> Romans8:1 *There is therefore now no condemnation*
> *to those who are in Christ Jesus, who do not*
> *walk according to the flesh, but*
> *according to the Spirit.*
> (NKJV)

Spiritual identity is important. God has already made a new thing and why don't you perceive it? Is it too good to be true? Do not question, just receive it. In 2 Corinthians 5:17 we are told that old things are passed away. That is another way of saying old things are dead. Gone. Never to be brought up again. Never ever, bring them up again. It is not by your works, it is for His sake. If you do not know who you are, you will desire what the pigs are eating, like the prodigal son, even when you are a prince or princess.

God's grace is sufficient to help you understand what may seem hard to grasp. You are a new being your level is far much higher than Daniel, Moses or Elijah. Am I being disrespectful to these great generals? No. Understand who you are and the times you live in.

> Matthew 11:11 *I tell you the truth: Among those born of women there has not risen anyone greater than John the Baptist; yet he who is least in the kingdom of heaven is greater than he.*
>
> (NIV)

John the Baptist is a great general, not even Moses could be compared to him. Amazing. From the Old Testament there are exceptions though. Could you think of the possibilities i.e. People who were not born of women? Answers are in the Bible. The greatest question which arises is this; **Dear Christian, are you born of a woman?** The correct perspective (answer) to this question is the key to your dominion. The least in the kingdom is greater than the greatest of the Old Testament. **Slow down**. You are about to slam into... into Holy Truth. It may sound unpalatable, but it is the real Word of God. What does this scripture mean? Are you born again? **Anyone who is born again is not born of 'woman' but of the Spirit of God.** When you are born again you are born from above. You are not earthly. You are born of the

Spirit. John 3:6. And you are born of God, **not woman!** Did you get it? The first time you were born, you were born of a woman. Your mama gave birth to you. Flesh gave birth to flesh.

> John 3:6 *Flesh gives birth to flesh,*
> *but the Spirit gives*
> *birth to spirit.*
> (NIV)

The second time you were born, it is different. Now hold your breath and read the next line very very slowly. **But the second could not be born without the first dying.** Fascinating. **The first person who was born is no more.** That is not some religious fantasy, that is the truth! **And without this truth, you are in boiling water.**

> John 1:13 *Which were born, not of blood, nor of the*
> *will of the flesh, nor of the will of*
> *man, but of God.*

You are not born of blood, your life is not in that human blood anymore. **Your blood line is not a factor.** Your human descent does not matter. How and where you were born is irrelevant. Your first birth does not matter what matters is your second! This limited human blood is no longer a factor in your life. Kenny, some wise person will tell you, you are suffering because you come from the line of weak people. Your father had this weakness. **Excuse me sir! Do you know my Father? Do you really know my Father?** We have seen a great rise in deliverance ministries.

Your human descent does not matter.

We have seen Christians being prayed for, every 20 seconds. These special demons are more powerful than the Holy Spirit. For the Holy Spirit seems to have resigned to fate. What is also very sweet about these deliverances is that it doesn't matter what you are doing, just go there and it will be sorted out. In fact there is a great dependence on the pastor or prophet. If you stole, the prophet tells you to take a certain item, use it and the judge will acquit you. Irresponsible behavior is encouraged. Steal, the man of God will sort it out. Prayerlessness is on the rise. We are rushing to be told what is going to happen in our lives. Pastor, what do you see? *I see you rich.* We have completely lost it. *Pastor I have a generational curse.* Generational curse? **Many who claim to have a generational curse don't even know what a generational curse is.** We will explain that in details later. You are born from above. Live it!

II. IDENTITY CONFIRMED

God is your Father and that truth must not be taken lightly. You are born again. It was not the weak or base desires of the flesh that brought you up. There is no question of legitimate or illegitimate child in Christ. All are legitimate. It is not man who decided that you should be born again, but God Himself. So I tell you again, you are superior to anyone in the Old Testament. *Uh you are kidding Keyworth.* I wish I was. That is why I encourage you not to move with a badge of 'sin', it is one way of weakening your walk with God.

> Hebrews 10:1 *For the law having a shadow of good things to come, and not the very image of the things, can never with those sacrifices which they offered year by year continually make the comers thereunto perfect. ² For then would they not have ceased to be offered? because that the worshippers once purged should have had no more conscience of sins. ³ But in those sacrifices there is a remembrance again made of sins every year.*

Look at this. The Law could not make Comers or worshippers **perfect**. That is why they never ceased to offer sacrifices in the Old Testament. But what about the Lamb that takes away the sins of the world? He had to offer one sacrifice once and for all. Hey that should tell you something. **You have been perfected.** You are perfect. It is 'nonsense' to be screaming, 'No one is perfect'. That is not humility or wisdom. Of course we know communication is not easy, but accept what the Bible says you really are. Do not be religious, be a Christian. Now look at this. If you are standing, please sit down. You are about to ram into Holy Truth. And it may hit you hard. Ready? Bang!!

Hebrews 10:2b *...the worshippers once purged should have had no more conscience of sins.*

Once purged you should have no more conscience of sins! *Uh pastor Keyworth, that is not humility, we are sinners.* **Speak for yourself.** Most Christians I have met have a 'sins conscience' than righteousness conscience. In fact where ever they go, they must see something wrong, not what is right. I remember a man of God who said, 'Look at that woman. These girls, this is evil, sin'. I looked at the girl and didn't see anything wrong. I responded, 'If a woman is beautiful it does not make her evil. That is not sin'. Come on what kind of thinking is that? When did beauty become sin? Then God is the first and worst sinner for He is beautiful.

Psalm 27:4 *One thing I have desired of the LORD, That will I seek: That I may dwell in the house of the LORD All the days of my life, To behold the beauty of the LORD, And to inquire in His temple.*
(NKJV)

At one point I was forced to sit down with one Guest Speaker, because he was more 'sin conscience' inclined than anything else. We went through the Bible verse by verse, line by line. The man jumped up. Then he poured out his deepest thoughts, things that he had never told any other person. He was liberated. **The best thing that Satan has ever stolen from the Church is not love, or unity, but righteousness.** So, it is not strange for Christians to behave 'unrighteous' for they are following the whispers from the dark pit of Hell that say 'Did God really say you are righteous?' **If you don't accept you are righteous it will be hard to live like Christ.** An unrighteous person cannot love anyone. An unrighteous person is self-willed. He will always rebel. He does not know what unity is. An unrighteous person is wicked. Never ever take the sacrifice of the Lord Jesus lightly. Satanists have to constantly placate the devil with a sacrifice. We are different. Don't bring Satanism in Christianity through false humility or false wisdom. **You are perfect.** Be conscious of who you are in Christ. If you are not, you will live like the devil in unrighteousness. Romans 6:6 tells us that since the old self is dead then sin has no power. Satan has no grip over you. A dead person is never responsive to the surrounding. It is impossible. Unless he just collapsed or fainted. If you are in Christ, you are dead to sin. Don't respond to the world system around you. You did not faint. You died.

> Romans 6:12 *Let not sin therefore reign in your mortal body, that ye should obey it in the lusts thereof. [13] Neither yield ye your members as instruments of unrighteousness unto sin: but yield yourselves unto God, as those that are alive from the dead, and your members as instruments of righteousness unto God.*

We are given the instances when sin can grip a person

✓ Romans 6:12 and

✓ Romans 6:13

In the former sin comes to you but it must get permission from you. The key word is 'Let'. Let means you are in control. It involves doing something willingly. You have a choice. You are not really hopeless. The latter means you go out making yourself available to it. You yield or present or parade yourself. To 'Present' is to simply offer. You are saying, 'Hey, sin here boy, come on come and get me'. Friend you have a very complex nature. You have victory over sin 100%. The reason you don't seem to experience victory is because you're offering yourself too many excuses. And you are listening too much to garbage. Instead of looking at how impossible it is to lead a sin free life, start reading scriptures that show just how possible it is. Perspective, remember? This is why they are bombarding us with sex images, insults, lowest grade morals in higher offices, in songs, films etc, so that we are weakened. They know we are strong! They are doing this repeatedly until we just give in and say after all everyone is doing it. Even if everyone is doing it, why should you become scum just because everyone has become scum?

> Psalm 119:9 *How can a young man keep his*
> *way pure? By living according*
> *to your word.*
> (NIV)

Ah. It says 'young man'. Young man is not referring to a male only but also to a female. Young refers to a 'babe'. One who is not yet mature. Replace the word 'young' with 'new'.

> Psalm 119:9 *How can a new man*
> *keep his way pure? By living*
> *according to your word.*
> (Paraphrased)

Human bodies need food to remain functional. You need the Word to remain alive. The new man lives on the Word. Go for the Word of God. 'Young' also refers to one who has no clear direction, a wanderer. It means someone who is being tossed to and fro. Remember Ephesians 4:14? Get the Word of God and you will cease being a wanderer, for it will give you direction in life. Is it possible?

Philippians 4:13 *I can do everything through Him who gives me strength.* (NIV)

Your nature is not of sin. Stop feeding it. Meditate on what you are in Christ Jesus. It is common sense, whatever you meditate on, **grows**. It becomes more real. The first Adam was a living soul, the second a spirit. The former is gone, you belong to the latter. That is your nature. Meditate on this. Get the scriptures and speak them. Think about them. People are falling into sin because they are listening to what Satan is saying. But look. To obey Satan or God it takes faith and effort. Pick yourself up, believe God and start chomping His Word. You are spiritually undernourished. Faith is not a problem. Whom you have faith in is what matters. We all have faith. **Even doubt is faith in a negative way.** If you say, I don't believe in miracles, that is faith. You believe but believe wrongly. Your faith instead of providing you with a miracle, it cancels the miracle. **What a waste of faith!**

If Satan comes to you and says you are not dead. How do you respond? *'Yes, I'm also not sure if I am dead.'* Good, you are a genius. He did the same with Adam and Eve. And the consequences are everywhere. He made them question what God had said. Satan alone convinced two first hand witnesses. *God help us.* Eve knew. Adam knew. But the devil a stranger convinced them. **You must know what you know.** Confirm your identity by accepting what God says about you in His Word! Don't be moved by every little speech from hell. Stand. Isn't it strange to see people who do not know what God says, arguing with those who know? There is nothing as complex as ignorance. It seems, ignorance takes many forms.

If you do not get this foundation work, all else will be in vain. Now learn about the power to get whatever you need, no matter what happens in your life. Then you can enjoy the full revelation of Satan's best kept secrets.

5.

CHRISTIANITY AND PERSISTENCE

^{Mark 11:12} *The next day as they were leaving Bethany, Jesus was hungry.* ¹³ *Seeing in the distance a fig tree in leaf, he went to find out if it had any fruit. When he reached it, he found nothing but leaves, because it was not the season for figs.* ¹⁴ *Then he said to the tree, "May no one ever eat fruit from you again." And his disciples heard him say it.*
(NIV)

A lot of God's children are in oppression and bondage because of one main factor, the lack of persistence. God's children give up easily.

✓ **Persistence by definition means things are not rosy.**

✓ **Persistence means there are opposing forces.**

✓ **Persistence means I am getting there despite...**

The Lord Jesus, the Great Grand Master of persistence gave us a grand lesson in this scripture. He came to a fig tree to look for figs. But He got nothing. Why didn't it bear fruit? **It was not the season for figs**. But Jesus did something that was appalling to the disciples. He cursed the tree.

I.   GOD'S PROFIT

Blown away by the shock of Jesus cursing the tree, Peter became enveloped in deep thoughts. *It is amazing that Jesus could do such a thing.* I fully understand the shock that came upon Peter. Jesus cursed a tree **for not bearing fruit out of season**. And the curse quickly took effect. That means Jesus meant what He said! But that is unfair, if that is how Jesus judges. How does He expect a tree to bear when it is not the season? Jesus was saying if I cannot profit from you, no one will. That is the other side of Jesus we have ignored, or we force ourselves to ignore. Jesus is the Lord of Profit. He wants it. That's why He teaches us to profit.

> Isaiah 48:17 *Thus saith the LORD, thy Redeemer, the Holy One of Israel;* ***I am the LORD thy God which teacheth thee to profit****, which leadeth thee by the way that thou shouldest go.*
> (Emphasis added)

God's children are so content with unproductive lives that it does not bother them if their semi-Christian lives affect Jesus or not.

Christians do not understand that Jesus is a serious Master and all who profess to follow Him must be serious. I will never forget the period 1994–95. I was praying around 10:00 pm, suddenly I saw a house on fire. The fire was very ferocious. Thick, aggressive flames destroying a house. Then the Lord spoke. **'This family has turned its back on me, I've sent judgment upon it. Go and warn them.'** Unbelievably today's theology has explained judgement out of the Bible, thanks to the devil's cunning nature. Dream on. The following day I took two other people with me and went to the place God had shown me. We found the house. Two men and a woman were seated outside. When they saw the Bibles, we were carrying, one of the men spoke, 'Young men you are evangelizing, that's good. Unfortunately everyone at this house is born-again.' I knew we were being *kindly* dismissed. There was light laughter.

'Actually we are not evangelizing. God has sent us to this house,' I responded.

'Young man, go back and listen from God properly,' the other man chipped in.

'If God speaks I don't have to go back. He is going to speak right here right now. We are not here for games. The Lord said He's sending judgment upon this house. We came to warn you,' I said.

'Keep quiet.' The woman told the husband and the friend before they could say another word. 'This is serious. Let's get in the house all of us.'

In fact, it was more of an order. I know that to speak like that she broke many rules in our African culture, but I saw godly fear in her. She sacrificed culture to please Jesus. Oh how I pray that we do not judge the vessels, but weigh the message and if it is really ours we accept it in humility. For if we have certain vessels that we expect God to send to us, we shall miss the times God has visited us. The husband and the friend became quiet as she led the way.

Describing the real situation later in the house, the woman of the house poured her heart out without reservation. She said she had stopped a long time ago being a Christian. The only reason she went to church on Sunday was because she had a position. Her husband had also lost interest in God. In addition, he had a *new life style* with *new friends*. She revealed how strange sores were licking up her husband's shanks and how one of her daughters had just developed a stiff neck, and she was lying in bed in her bedroom. I prayed for the daughter who was instantly healed. I prayed with the man and his wife and their friend. **The room was filled with the tangible presence of God.** The man of the house wept. When he finished crying he had a certain look on his face. When a man has connected to God the Lion of Judah arises in him. I could see the enemy had fled. He looked around the room and said, 'Let's pray.' He prayed so powerfully. We were all moved. The tangible presence of God was even greater. Friend

I do not know if you had fallen or not. Jesus does not condemn you. Get up. The power of God was upon that man in a mighty way. There was something about that man and God. I know there is something about you and God. Come back to God today. Many people know about God, but few know His heart. I urge you to return to God today. He is expecting you.

Encouraged, restored and blazing with new life, the man of the house spoke, 'We need more young men like you who can listen to what God is saying. Thank you for saving our lives.' It wasn't long (a few months later) I met the friend of the man.

'Man of God, people should listen when God is speaking. They should respect men of God. That family God sent you to, there is disaster!'

'What?!' I was shocked. Everything was alright when we left the place. I went there and death greeted me. Four members of that family gone in two months. That's on average a funeral every two weeks. Even the man of the house was also dead! But the wife was alive. God sent me to the woman a few years later to tell her to change her ways too. He told me to tell her to make a decision in 7 days. Before the seven days elapsed, she saw me in town and changed direction. It's like I was the trouble maker. But God, who is great, had spoken to that woman's daughter in another town, to tell her family to turn to Jesus seriously. The day I told the woman about the seven days her daughter was present. She had traveled to warn her family too. Do not look at the vessel. Get the message. You think you know your daughter or your son? Think again. You don't. You remember the nappies and the mess. This is a spirit being now. When a person is born he is born as flesh. When a person is born-again the person becomes a spirit being. John 3:6. May God deliver us from familiarity. Familiarity is killing more people than the devil is. This story has been going on in Livingstone in another version: an angel appeared in Livingstone and pronounced judgment upon a certain family. Actually people have told this version from an eye witness–point–of–view. It has been well spiced.

Fighting the grace of God upon your life is disastrous. Jesus is your only help, but if you flee from His presence, the devil will be more than glad to receive you on the other side. The seven–day period had expired. **Three days later i.e. on the tenth day just after coming back from work, the woman sat on a chair and died. Just like that.** I never knew what would happen after the seven days. But I learned my lesson. We should never take the Love of Jesus for granted. If we say, He is our Saviour, then let Him be Lord too. You cannot have one and not the other. My point is not to infuse fear in you, but for you to check your life and live for Him. We are here for Him. We must not give up. Let us keep on doing good. Always remember that. Am I pointing an accusing finger? God forbid. I wouldn't dare. My prayer and hope is that as we talk about the **love** of God we do not lose the **reverence**!

Hebrews 12:28 *Wherefore we receiving a kingdom which cannot be moved, let us have grace, whereby we may serve God acceptably with reverence and godly fear:* *29 For our God is a consuming fire.*

Familiarity breeds contempt. Contempt always brings disaster. Without God we are nothing. Let us serve Him **acceptably** with **reverence** and **godly fear**.

God hates excuses. Through this example of the fig tree, our Lord told His disciples, that include you and me, to be productive always. Do not be complacent because of the conditions (seasons). There is nothing impossible with you. Child of God yesterday was the last day you gave excuses for not following the leading of the Holy Spirit. And it was the last day Satan oppressed you. The word 'oppression' is very ugly. It means **fraud**. Satan should never steal from you. The devil is not as great as he is portrayed. Here is something to think about.

II. GOD'S AUTHORITY

✓ Only The Poor Steal.

The devil is poor. It doesn't matter how you are perceived in society whether a big shot or not. If you steal you are poor.

✓ One Can Only Steal From The 'Haves'

Has the devil stolen from you? You 'have'. You are rich.

✓ One Can Only Steal From The Ignorant 'Haves'.

May you refuse to be ignorant anymore. The devil is poor, you are rich. Ignorance is gone. Are you ready to change your life by His Word? Let us look at one scripture that will change your life forever if you are ready. Read the following scripture slowly and be ready to learn one or two things from it. Put the devil where he belongs.

> Luke 10:19 *Behold, I give unto you* **power** *to tread on* **serpents** *and* **scorpions**, *and over all the* **power** *of the enemy: and* **nothing shall by any means hurt you**.
> (Emphasis added)

There is no authority above the one you have. Serpents and scorpions are classes of demons, they are all under your feet. Halleluiah. But that is warm up. Now here is where you don't blink. You don't even breathe. Hold your breath. Jesus the Master of the universe has given you power. The first 'power' in this scripture means ability and authority. It means you are in control. The second power means Satan's army. But we could be specific and say Jesus has given us authority over all **occult miraculous power.** Yes over **OCCULT MIRACULOUS POWER**. Interesting! I want you to think of any occult power that has left you inebriated. Think of the great machinery of secret societies and how they have covered over 99% (arguably) of world takeover. Still what you have is above them.

'Is this reality Pastor Keyworth?'

'Yes Jane, the lie is what you have been living.'

The word 'tread' means to step on. We are to step on the serpents and scorpions. Not the other way round! God has given us authority over **snakes (serpents) and scorpions**. Are we doing that? Let us dissect these two words, 'serpents' and 'scorpions'.

A. SERPENTS

A closer look at the word 'serpent' shows us that this is a personal characteristic of Satan. 'Serpent' is the cunning nature or **quality** of Satan. After studying or observing then he comes craftily for a kill. He comes in the name of peace, but inside he is a volcano of bitterness. What is the Lord Jesus saying in this scripture, Luke 10:19? Do you remember what happened to Adam and Eve? **Satan was able to study them. But Jesus is saying what happened to Adam and Eve will not happen to you!** When you talk about this serpent character, you are talking about the quality to deceive. Has the devil deceived you? The false financial down turns, the false fuel shortages and ensuing high prices, the manufactured economic failings, political super heroes, the humble looking devils masquerading as men of the cloth etc. Are you treading on serpents? How much of your guard have you let down? If you want to be the friend of the world, God will not be your friend. But when you are alert, though they dance around, they will not fool you. Vonetta, do you understand? Don't be short–sighted. Assimilate this. The devil is shuddering as you take it in. This is one of the devil's closely guarded secrets. He does not want you to know this. Please pray that this gets into your spirit not just your head. The serpent studied Adam and Eve and came craftily for them, but this must not happen to you.

John 3:8 *The wind blows wherever it pleases. You hear its sound, but you cannot tell where it comes from or where it is going. So it*

*is with everyone born
of the Spirit."*
(NIV)

Jesus clearly stated it is impossible to study one who is born again! **The devil cannot tell what is going to happen next in your life. You are unpredictable!** That is what the scripture is saying. The one who is born again is led by the Holy Spirit. For the devil to fully study him, he must first study the Holy Spirit who leads him.

And no finite mind can comprehend the Infinite. In John 1:5, it is written that Darkness can neither comprehend nor eliminate you. How can it study you? This is great news. Defeat is not for you.

But 'serpents' could also imply human instruments working under the influence of these spirits. The word 'nothing' means 'No one, no person, no scheme, man or woman, no weapon or spells' can harm you. **It does not matter who backs them, what matters is who backs you!** 'Serpents' are not ordinary pickpocket demons. These are **Planners**. These demons directly control certain people for many nefarious schemes to be enforced on earth today. Yes a lot of wicked plans are in motion, and many blind people are either accepting them unquestionably or do not even know there are such things. Ignorance is fatal. Jesus is on our side. Yes. Should we talk about what the devil is doing? It's common sense if it's a real war you are in, you have to. When Jesus gave us authority over serpents, what He was giving us is authority over **all the plans** of the devil! (*That just passed over your head like an F 15*). Don't you miss this Word. It is yours. No demonic plan can work against you and succeed. In other words, Jesus was saying you have the control, you can frustrate the devil's plans against you. Halleluiah. Luke 10:19 is the New Testament version of

Isaiah 8:10 Devise your strategy, but it will be thwarted; propose your plan, but it will not stand, for God is with us.

(NIV)

Isaiah8:10 Take counsel together, but it will come to nothing; Speak the word, but it will not stand, For God is with us."

(NKJV)

Isaiah 8:10 Call your councils of war, but they will be worthless. Develop your strategies, but they will not succeed. For God is with us!"

(NLT)

I do not know where we got this idea of devil's sitting down after careful research on us, strategizing and finishing us off. That is the devil's gospel. There is no such luck for him. It's pure gloom for the devil. He has really lost weight. Every time he fails to destroy God's child he has to come up with a lie to explain to his followers so that they do not realize he is not as big as he claims. His mouth aches. How many lies is he going to manufacture? No matter what the devil devises again you, it must come to disaster for him. It will not work. **God is with us** is a New Testament revelation. No matter what version you use it is clear the devil's war council has been cancelled by Emmanuel! Halleluiah!!! **Emmanuel, God is with us does not just mean Jesus walking on earth with the disciples in the Bible. No. It means in its fullest sense, Jesus living in you by His Spirit, the Holy Spirit. The fulfillment of this Word is right now in your life!**

Matthew 1:23 *Behold, a virgin shall be with child, and*
Shall bring forth a son, and they shall call
his name Emmanuel, which being
interpreted is, God
with us.

There is no time when a child of God is alone and defenseless. Impossible. The devil wants you to think otherwise. Now let us look at the thwarting part. To thwart is to spoil, frustrate or put an end to. It is to cancel! Is the message getting into you? But how do you spoil? If you are born again the Word is vital. Stand on the authority that comes from your understanding of the Word. There is authority in the Word. When you know the truth, fix your heart on it. David in Psalm 57: 7 said his heart was fixed. Your heart must be also. I call it **'Locking On'**. When you have got a revelation and a target never let any devil distract you. Go for it with all of your being. Lock on!

Biblical truth states, a person who moves in spiritual authority is the one who really believes. Exercise your faith. Faith without works is dead. The scriptures say this throughout the Bible. The Apostle Paul put it more powerfully when he said the Gospel is not in word but in demonstration. When you quote scriptures against the devil's plans, they fall off, read on to understand the principles that govern the world you live in. Understanding is important. **Do you know that canceling the devil's plans through declaration of God's Word stops them from manifesting?** Friend I would like to share with you a serious secret of the underworld. **The underworld operates on HPT, Host–Parasite Technique.** Every human being is a potential host.

Every human being must be under a demonic spell or torture. Every person in the underworld must have a host! What does that mean? Whether you are a Christian or not, someone somewhere will offer you to the demons as a sacrifice. That's why some people have problems they don't understand. Misfortunes will come your way so that, someone somewhere will benefit. This has nothing to do with race or colour. If you didn't know, welcome to the kingdom of darkness. And one had better perform or else he or she becomes the host! And hosts are expendable. These fellas have the ability to cast spells by declaring them. They speak, and those spells will come and affect your life. This is when you take a stance. It is not up to God to do that. It is up to you. Satanists speak words that carry spells. But you can cancel those words with yours. They can speak but you can speak much much better. Fight or fall.

> Isaiah8:10 *Take counsel together, but it will*
> *come to nothing; Speak the word,*
> *but it will not stand, For*
> *God is with us."*
> (NKJV)

The Word is important because it reveals the devil's limits. Not only that, it also reveals his intentions.

Child of God no devil can outwit you. Let us get to 2 Kings 6:8–12. Elisha could tell what Ben Hadad spoke in his bedroom! In the name of Jesus, you are victorious! No plan can work. The devil is a persistent fool, you must know dear. And as God's child, you must not have short–range focus. Never give up. **What time did the king send his army?** In the night. The devil thinks he is the master of the **night**. Do not be a seasonal Christian. There must never be seasons when you are spiritually off. Be evergreen. Stop getting ready and live ready. Jesus is the same yesterday, today and forever. Jesus taught us that through the fig tree. Unlike the fig tree, keep bearing without excuses like the Tree of Life. The greatness of God must be revealed in you all the time. Persistence is the key to unlocking the impossible. **Never let circumstances change your Christianity, but let your Christianity change your circumstances.**

Did the Syrian army know it was walking into an ambush? I doubt it. But one thing is clear for sure. Elisha is no ordinary man. That is why the king sent a big army to capture him. He was respected. What was Elisha's response? **By his word he struck them blind.** Learn to discomfit the enemy plans against you by your word. What does it mean to be blind? To lose vision. The devil can lose his vision of destroying you now! What we see in Elisha's life is supposed to be your way of life as a Christian, do you know this, Verona? **Unfortunately, there has been a reversal of positions.** I think most Christians are upside down! If you see a thief chasing the police, surely things are upside down! The devil now knows our every move and discussion. *We are doing great.* In your life you could have been experiencing certain difficulties. Whatever you do seems to be known by the enemy. **That is the spirit of clairvoyance.**

Christians have the capacity by the power of the Holy Spirit to bind and render ineffective the spirit of clairvoyance! **Satan has counterfeited the Word of Knowledge to the point that he even has clairaudience. Here is an extra tip. I know this is going to mess up your appetite.** Some clergy are using this spirit of clairvoyance and clairaudience to know what you are planning and doing. The idea is to make you have more confidence in them and finally make you vulnerable to their swindling. You unknowingly are their host. They are parasites. **By the power of the Holy Spirit and in the Name of Jesus Christ of Nazareth, the Son of the Living God make all of them blind and deaf!** If that is the power in your pastor's life it will stop operating effectively in your presence. Child of God learn these secrets and put the devil to flight. He will never like you. The devil's counterfeit powers are no match for us. Are you seeing the devil's covert operations? The Holy Ghost will reveal whatever,

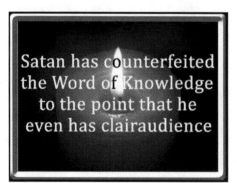

Satan has counterfeited the Word of Knowledge to the point that he even has clairaudience

the devil has prepared on his agenda. Listen. You can never stop the devils from planning against you, but you can stop their plans before they mature. **They can plan, but you can crush.** Your middle name is Crusher!

B. SCORPIONS

A serious scrutiny of the word 'scorpion' reveals that this is the **quality** of Satan to **penetrate** or **pierce** your **armor** or defense mechanism. But there is one thing he cannot pierce, unless you want him to, **your shield of faith.** Understand this; while the first are war planners or strategists, these are attackers. Scorpions do not come to 'sweet talk'. They attack. Jesus said all their attacks would be thwarted. Saint, are you getting this? Scorpions stand for **attacks**. But you can change all this. Let us read it this way:

*I have given you authority to **cancel** or*
***frustrate all plans** and*
***attacks** of the*
enemy

The Old Testament version concerning attacks says

Isaiah 54:17a *no weapon forged*
against you will
prevail ...,"
(NIV)

Is that sinking in you? I want to see the devil admitted to the hospital tomorrow because of you. When the doctor asks him,

'What happened devil?'

His response, 'I was hit by a missile called........(your name)

Doctor shaking his head, 'Fatal mistake '

Devil, 'Huh, Doc. You're even putting it lightly. I was history'

Doctor, 'Lucky you escaped'

Devil, 'All the luck of hell was upon me. Barely escaped. From now on I'm changing towns. I didn't know some fellas would understand and implement 1 John 2:6. They are torturing me the way He did'.

Believe it or not there is **no plan or attack** against you that can prevail. Witchcraft included. Spells from these spiritual serpents that people invoke against you will not work. **You are beyond defeat**. It does not matter how you feel on Tuesday. What you declared on Monday stands. Maintain it. The Lord Jesus said that even the devil's **entire force or occult miraculous powers** (remember the meaning of the second 'power' in Luke 10:19?) can never hurt you. In fact, Jesus used emphasis to show the impossibility of you being **defeated** in this scripture.

✓ Nothing shall by any means hurt you means **never, never** shall you be hurt or defeated.

✓ Nothing shall by **any** means hurt you means there is no **method** or **trick** that can succeed against you. A fellow on the street today would say, **'I swear, I truly swear nothing will harm you!'**

But this look at the impact of the Word, the authority you get from the Word and the spiritual gift of the Word of Knowledge does not tell the whole story. It is warm up. There is another very important thing, though heavily criticized, ignored and abused. Let us courageously look at this great topic...

III. GOD'S WISDOM

A. TONGUES!

> 1 Corinthians 12:28 *And God hath set...in the church... diversities of tongues.*

A lot of dust has been raised over this issue. But there is no need. Though it is quite understandable. Some people who talked so much about tongues have fallen into the devil's trap. Their beginning was great, but along the way most of them, were either bought or they abandoned their first love to embrace another god, that which cannot love them back. Knowing the kind of damage they did to him, the devil quickly enlisted some of these great people and grafted them into the core of his elite system. It is shameful and regrettable that people who championed tongues have fallen to the devil who once dreaded them. *The kings have bowed to their subordinate.* Confusion has arisen over tongues even among tongue-speakers. I witnessed pastors forcing people to speak in tongues. Telling them the tongues (words) they should speak. *Say, 'Blah' Now say, 'Kadoo'.* It is such kind of recklessness that many condemn. God the Holy Spirit is the one who is in charge. You don't force anyone to speak. That is deception! Apart from that there are those who become uncontrollable when they start speaking in tongues. That is not right either. The Holy Spirit does not take your brains out when you speak in tongues. Tongues do not show how spiritual you are. You could speak in tongues and still be a useless fellow. It is important to understand tongues and to understand who the Holy Spirit is. Today's average Christian, am sorry to say, does not know the Holy Spirit. No wonder 'other holy spirits' have come in and we don't seem to notice the difference. I am not exaggerating, satanists have a snake they call the **Holy Spirit**. Be careful.

Believers must know the underlying issues concerning tongues. Understand why certain people oppose tongues. Some are legitimate concerns while others are purely devilish. Most people in the kingdom of man (earth) are very ignorant about tongues. Of the three kingdoms, two of them are privileged to have the secrets of this gift. The Kingdom of God and the Kingdom of Satan. Now get this. God's Kingdom has tongues (diversities, various or many kinds) given by God The Holy Spirit. And the devil's kingdom also speaks in tongues, but these are demonic tongues. In the devil's kingdom, tongues are a settled issue. They don't discuss, but just implement. They 'chant', speak volubly, they 'hiss'. They know the effect of tongues. **Some things can never be accomplished in Satanism unless one speaks in tongues, did you know that? There is a level in devil worship when demons will not respond to any human language unless tongues.**

Beloved, tongues are ours as God's children. But what do we do? We debate, hold seminars, meanwhile cemeteries are being filled with Satan's victims. What Satanists have are counterfeit. Using this New Age tactic the devil has counterfeited the Church to the point one can hardly see the difference between the true and the false. Coupled with unrestrained freedom, total confusion in the Church, many are ready to conclude, tongues are false. Tongues don't exist. Friend, tongues are real. Yes the Church has been careless. The Church has been counterfeited. Some of our leaders have been and others still are, in the devil's kingdom. But we will not throw away what is right just because someone counterfeited it. Let us quickly touch this subject, for without it the Church will remain on the ropes being pummeled like a helpless boxer in the 12th Round. It is in the last Round, the 12th when you go for the kill. If you mess it up in the final round, you are going home without the belt. Your beginning could have been great, but if the finish is terrible, you are useless. The beginning does not matter, but the end does. You can start small, it is not a sin. But ending small is a sin. Don't despise small beginnings, but small endings? Unbiblical.

Basically, there are two major categories of tongues, which could be split further into six. I am just introducing, make your own study. The basic definition of biblical tongues is, a language not naturally acquired. In English this means, tongues are supernatural. There are –

1. PRIVATE TONGUES

Am interested in you getting the picture. The name does not matter, some people would call them personal, others devotional. Private tongues could be split into four.

a) Personal Build.

> 1 Corinthians 14:14 *"For if I pray in a tongue, my spirit prays, But my mind is unfruitful,"* (NIV)

All they do is build your spiritual man, your spirit. Nothing diffuses satanic forces like continuous life of speaking in tongues. This language no devil understands it. This is a direct line to God Almighty and no devil can tell what is happening. It is a secret code of special intimacy with God. This is the only kind that God has given you a *'switch'* for. You can speak anytime anywhere. **This is the kind every child of God must have.**

But it must quickly be pointed out that there is also an element of speaking angelic language(s). This is the second private tongue.

> 1 Corinthians 13:1 *"If I speak in the tongues … of angels..."*
> (NIV)

In this case you **could be** addressing angels. You are not praying to angels, but as co–workers, you 'strategize' together.

> Hebrews 1:13 *...the angels...[14] Are they not all*

ministering spirits, sent forth to
minister for them who
shall be heirs of
salvation?

The holy angels and you are working to accomplish God's wonderful plan for humankind. You are part of God's great army. This angelic language(s) I believe the devil can hear since he is a fallen angel. It is **also possible** when you speak in an angelic language you are praising God and declaring the great wonders of God before the angelic host. Hebrews 12:22–23. But when Satanists and spiritists speak in tongues they speak to particular demons to carry out certain assignments to achieve their wicked desires. **I repeat, certain demons will never respond to earthly languages.** That is a secret Satan has tried to hide under his pillow. Of course this service from demons comes at a price, a fatal price. They pay dearly for it! Tongues are not a joke. Tongues in Satan's kingdom are indispensable. **Some people who oppose tongues know what they are doing. When they say, 'What is this nonsense of tongues?' The dull ones chortle, not knowing they are being drained of their capacity to fight the good fight of faith. Real tongues cause great havoc in Satan's kingdom!** Don't be fooled.

Christians should also realize that they cannot only speak in tongues, but also **sing** in tongues. This is the third private tongue.

1 Corinthians 14:15 *What is it then? I will pray with the*
spirit, and I will pray with the understanding
also: I will sing with the spirit,
and I will sing with the
understanding
also…

Speak and sing in tongues, your spiritual life will soar to greater heights. So, focus and do not look back. You probably know this already; many a child of God leads life carelessly. There is no consistency when they start something. Satan goes on leave when he sees Christians going to attend crusades or 'meetings' that put them on 'fire'. He knows that two weeks down the line, there will not be even embers to show there ever was a fire! The worldly language is back—all the negative confessions, evil speaking and prayerlessness. No Bible reading and study. Fighting one another becomes rife. It is more shocking beyond what 30 million defibrillators can do. Christians always cursing fellow Christians and calling them demon possessed.

Can God answer their prayers like this? It is with great shock I have come to realize that many Christians want witchcraft not Christianity. **Christianity with power but no love is witchcraft.** Many seek only the power. The miracles are what they are going for. *I want a miracle. I want a miracle.* Dear you are misguided. Yes God will give you power, but do you know how lasting power comes? **Power is a by–product of intimacy with God.** Don't go for the by product, you will be a by Christian. No wonder people cannot tell between God's miracles and the devil's. How can you tell if all you want is power not the relationship? Do not lose your first love. The more you speak in tongues the more you flow in the love for Jesus and the love for other people. You must never have classes of people you love and people you hate. I mean that literally. If you speak in tongues but have no love you are wasting your time. Shut up. You should not hate other believers because they are your family. And you must not hate the unbelievers because you are sent to them. They are potential family. My spiritual father once told me, 'Key the only light of love other people may ever see in life is you. You witness more by your life than by your words.' Mature love has to be emphasized in the body of Christ.

Christian love must be emphasized. Maturity is imperative. We are playing circus. Some people think their lives are more important than that of others. Superstar Christians. Listen, let me help you. You do not have to wait for judgment day to know your verdict. **You are deceived.** A person who does not love others is not yet born again. Period. Am sorry if this is your situation. Get a life! Selfishness won't help you. It's for low lives.

> John 15:12 *My command is this: Love each other as I have loved you.*
> *¹³ Greater love has no one than this, that he lay*
> *down his life for his friends. ¹⁴ You are*
> *my friends if you do what*
> *I command.*

Did you see that? You did? What does it say? Jesus is dying for us. Wonderful. Clap for yourself. Christianity is sweet as long as Jesus is doing all the dying while we watch from the big screen, flicking through the channels. Let us flip the coin. Are you ready? Do you love others to the point of dying for them? *'Uh this fella has lost it. He is turning us into Kamikaze. Jesus died for us we should not die for one another.'* That sounds like wisdom, but when weighed, it is sensual, worldly and demonic. Wisdom is seen by her children. **Friend, let me tell you the real reason you do not want to die for another person. It is not because Jesus died for everyone, but because you think your life is more valuable than another person's life is. You are super selfish. And with Satan's ego.** *I hope you are not twins.* And that my friend, if you have never been told, is the foundation of **Satanism**. In Satanism, your life is more valuable than another's is. The very Word we preach has cost someone his or her life for you to have it. Many, whom Jesus died for have died for this gospel to go on.

> 1 John 3:16 *Hereby perceive we the love of God, because he*
> *laid down his life for us: and we ought to*
> *lay down our lives for the*
> *brethren.*

Jesus loved the Church, the Bride to the point of death and how does the Bride respond? By courageously being ready if need be, to die for Him. It is spiritual Romeo and Juliet. Revelation 12:11. And did you notice that sacrificial love is a command? **Anyway, you can only die for that which is valuable; you know what**

is valuable to you. And have you seen that you need to lay your life down for the brethren in 1 John 3:16? Allow me to add this: A friend, who is a farmer in USA, told me that pigs fear to die, but sheep do not. Friend, to bring the Word of God to you undiluted, we put our lives on the line. We treasure you. You are worth dying for, that's why we put our all on the line just for you. We are not stunt men or women, we love you genuinely. Nobody in this age will love you the way we do. They all want a piece of you. But we want peace for you. To some we have nothing better to do. We don't love ourselves and our families, really?

Do you understand now when we say no one person's life is more important than another's is? It is only in the other kingdom where people think their lives are more valuable than their friends' are. Christianity gives no such room; in fact, you consider others better and love them as Jesus loved us, to the point of death. *Keyworth, are you saying you can literally die for another person today?* Beloved, God has never taught me any other love apart from that kind of love. I say a very big YES! Jesus is my witness. And even the devil acknowledges it! I may not be strong in other areas, but on that, God has given me the grace. May the Mighty Holy Spirit kill that spirit of selfishness in you today, in the name of Jesus! May you stop being crooked. May you stop being jealous. May you start considering others better and of greater value than you. May you stop using people for your selfish gain. Begin to love. Love people. Love God. There are so many people who are even old today, who have never known what love is. They smile, seem happy, but very much hating and hurting. Couples. Enduring each other. Experience the real love of Jesus. Real love is real. Satanism is founded on selfishness. Christianity on love. May God's Word pierce your heart right now and destroy that selfishness in the Name of Jesus Christ of Nazareth! A Christian's life starts with death then resurrection. Why? One of the reasons is that selfishness is very deceptive. The old self does not know that it is selfish. God wants the old self dead. Romans 6:6.

b) Personal Safety

Romans 8:26 *Likewise the Spirit also helpeth our infirmities: for we know not what we should pray for as we ought: but the Spirit itself maketh intercession for us with groanings which cannot be uttered.*

As you are being built up in your spirit, you become more aware of the leading of the Spirit of God. **Have you ever had a strong urge to pray for a particular person at a particular time, sometimes at an odd time?** The urge is very strong and when you try to pray only tongues come out? I call these Personal Safety or Counter Attack Tongues —CAT. This is the fourth kind of tongues. While you have a *'switch'* to speak in the first one, the Personal Build, you do not have it here. These tongues do not occur all the time. They happen when someone is in danger or something unfavorable is about to happen. They crush or frustrate the attacks of the enemy. Usually a confirmation accompanies these tongues. If you find out someone will tell you how he or she, for example, escaped a fatal accident at a particular time, and it is exactly the time you prayed. **I have witnessed the miraculous, numerous times, in this area.** Sometimes the Holy Spirit just gives you the urge to pray in tongues. Afterwards you will realize you prayed for another Christian who was in danger. If there is a gift that binds the Body of Christ together, it's the gift of tongues! The reason the Holy Spirit never told you may be due to your lack of maturity. Maybe you hate that brother or sister. God used you like Balaam's donkey. Grow up. Move in love. You can never be a Christian and not love the way He loves.

At other times, you can just wake up from sleep and find you are already speaking in tongues. Your spirit is alert and the Holy Spirit has already started the spiritual generator. Dear, we are complex! The first kind of tongues builds you up and frustrates the **plans** of the enemy, while the second fends off direct **attacks**.

2. PUBLIC TONGUES

There are two categories here.

a) Ministerial–Evangelistic Tongues

> Acts 2:4 *And they were all filled with the Holy Ghost, and began to speak with other tongues, as the Spirit gave them utterance.*
> *⁵ And there were dwelling at Jerusalem Jews, devout men, out of every nation under heaven.⁶ Now when this was noised abroad, the multitude came together, and were confounded, because that every man heard them speak in his own language.*

A person will supernaturally speak an earthly language in public. The number of these tongues is according to the number of languages on earth. See 1 Corinthians 13:1a. This language is unknown to the speaker and the interpreter is usually the intended target. Here the Holy Spirit enables someone who does not know Korean for example to speak it, because there is someone whose attention the Lord wants to get. It is the Christian's 'burning bush' today. This is what the first Disciples experienced in the Book of Acts. People will draw near and as they do this, the Gospel of the Lord Jesus brings life to them. The Gospel of the Lord of the universe carries power. The miraculous happen. Tongues are part of the vocal miracles of the Gospel. Sermons (sermons yes are supernaturally loaded with His saving power, delivering power, healing power etc) and prophecy being others. You do not have a 'switch' for this kind of tongue. It is frequent in evangelistic meetings or encounters.

b) Ministerial Prophetic Tongues

1 Corinthians 12:10 *To another the working of miracles; to another prophecy; to another discerning of spirits; to another divers kinds of tongues; to another the interpretation of tongues*

A look at this scripture shows that this is an office. This is where some think 'Tongues' are not for everyone. The truth is very clear. **Tongues are for everyone. There are diversities of tongues.** It depends on which tongues you are talking about. An interpreter accompanies this one and it could be, either the speaker or another person who flows in a similar ministry. The purpose is to encourage the Church, give direction or reveal something. All in all the saints should benefit from the insight the Holy Spirit is giving.

Be encouraged that with tongues at your disposal no devil can **plan** against you and succeed. A person who was practicing Satanism gave up her trade when the person she was targeting, destroyed 'all her demonic paraphernalia' as he prayed in tongues. Before this, she had never encountered a Christian that strong. When I heard that testimony, I was an eye witness when she gave it, my mind went into overdrive. It's like God was speaking to me saying, 'It's because Christians are not demonstrating the Christian life why My name is being put to shame'. Romans 2:24. It is time to ask for forgiveness. Some people in the occult are perishing not because they want to, but there are no enough examples. Will you be an example today?

Christians must not belittle tongues. **They are the difference between dominion and depression.** Tongues are foolishness to some people. But it is in the foolish things that God has put His Wisdom. The words of the apostles Paul and Barnabas ring deafeningly

Acts 13:46b *...Since you reject it and do not*

*consider yourselves worthy of eternal
life, we now turn to the
Gentiles .* (NIV)

Doctor Luke puts it in a spectacular way. It has 'special effects'. He says:

Luke 7:30a *But the Pharisees and experts in
the law rejected God's purpose
for themselves...*

How in the world do you reject God's Purpose or Will for you? And what in the world do you remain with after rejecting His Will? It is not God who disqualifies. People do not consider themselves worthy of eternal life. Those who have this life should also understand what they have. **Eternal life is not just quantity or longevity of life, but also quality of life.** It is not God, but your personal decision that disqualifies you from receiving the total package. It is up to you to frustrate every demonic plan and cancel every attack. **Frustration, confusion and depression are demonic qualities. It is the devil's character. It is how he feels after failing to destroy Jesus and how he feels towards you because God has given you more than he can imagine**.

Do not share in his character. I refuse to be depressed in the name of Jesus. Depression is foreign to Christianity. In fact, it's me who depresses the enemy. I refuse to trade my superior position for the devil's pit, self–pity. I remember my teacher of Mathematics used to say there are three factors that make great Mathematicians. **A great Mathematician needs Confidence: confidence makes you believe you can do it. It makes you believe it is not tough, it can be done.** I totally agreed with him. Even as a Christian, I have come to notice that without confidence you cannot do anything. Confidence, the Bible says has great rewards.

Hebrews 10:35 *So do not throw away your*

confidence; it will be richly
rewarded. (NIV)

Confidence is richly rewarded, not poorly rewarded. Never throw it away. No matter what the devil throws at you never throw away confidence. David never lost it, even when people insulted him and said he was proud. God knows your heart; do not let man dissuade you. I have noticed that people who have no confidence mostly desire to shoot down the confidence of others. In fact they will shoot down any suggestion you come up with. They will tell you all the ways and reasons why it cannot work, but not a single way it can be done. Run away from such. Leave those who are always belittling you. You have nothing in common. The other thing that the teacher told us is **that *a real mathematician is Accurate.*** The man was right. You cannot be making the same mistakes over and over.

Eliminate the things that keep you down. And try different approaches, but do not be content making the same low class results. If I am given one plus two, and I write my answer as six, I will not write six again when the teacher has already told me it is wrong.

Hebrews 12:1 *Therefore, since we are surrounded by such a great cloud of witnesses,*
let us throw off everything that hinders and the
sin that so easily entangles, and let us run with
perseverance the race marked
out for us. (NIV)

Accuracy is a matter of attitude and understanding. Understand what you are doing and put everything in it. Where you keep on stumbling over the same issue, humble yourself and **SCREAM FOR HELP!!!** It is important to realize that some times what makes people not to ask for help is pride. A brother in the Lord told me this story. He was a good swimmer. And that sweet afternoon, girls were all over the swimming pool. *We thank the Lord for girls.* He dove in and everybody cheered (especially the girls).

He couldn't really remember what happened, but he felt very tired and he knew he wasn't going to make it to the other side of the pool. He struggled like a good swimmer, but his energy was ebbing away at a terrific speed. Finally, he said if I shout for help, I will be the most embarrassed being in the universe. He was afraid of what the girls would say. So he gave up. He decided to give up and drown! (He narrated this to me). As his legs were giving in to his weight, he realized he had already reached the shallow side of the pool. He waded out of the pool. This was not the wisest of things to do, but we can all learn something from it.

Every real man struggles to ask for help. In fact, it takes a real man, all he has in himself to ask for help. Therefore, when a man comes to me with a request, it needs urgent attention; he is at the end of his tether. *I will deliberately forget to talk about those who have made a career out of asking for help. Those are mere imitations of men.* The third principle my teacher mentioned was **Speed**. *A mathematician is not slow*. Time wasting has been costing many Christians invaluable achievement. Some people are poor or suffering because they have a gift which they have shelved and they are waiting for the second coming of the Lord Jesus. Your blessing is in what God has given you to do. Broaden your vision.

Matthew 25:14 *"Again, it will be like a man going on a journey, who called his servants and entrusted his property to them.*[16] *The man who had received the five talents went at once and put his money to work and gained five more.* (NIV)

God has not called you to self, but to bless the world. Think of the ways you could reach out to people, then your blessings will begin flowing. In this parable

✓ The gift is from the master

✓ The responsibility of growth (multiplication) is the servants'

✓ The profit is the master's.

Note that the master knew their capacity to multiply what he gave them. You have the capacity to do it. Grace is upon you. What made the two wise servants manage to double the profit?

Passion is something worth living for. Passion is also something worth dying for.

They went at once. Time is a factor! As I exercised these principles and taught others, I came to add one factor. **Passion.**

Passion is not something you can make someone easily understand. It is hard to define, but this is how I define it.

✓ **Passion is something worth living for.**

✓ **Passion is also something worth dying for.** You feel it. It is in you. It is all over you. **There is no substitute for passion**.

✓ **Passion can make you endure the impossible**.

✓ **Passion is never intimidated**.

✓ **Passion is not afraid of shame**.

✓ **Passion keeps your thirst alive**.

✓ **Passion is a flame that others will see from afar. You do not tell them, they see it. Only a person with passion will have something to say. Because he speaks his entire being.**

✓ **Passion does not give up.**

✓ **Passion is *good* madness! No matter how many times**

the devil pours water on the flames of passion, the fire rekindles.

The devil has come to understand what all fire fighters have come to know, not all kinds of fire can be quenched by water. The other word for passion is zeal. Every day the fires of zeal burn brighter and they could go on blazing a century from today.

> John 2:17 *His disciples remembered that it is written: "Zeal for your house will consume me."* (NIV)

Persistence with all the necessary principles in place takes you to the top. Only those who endure to the end shall be saved. It is my hope you will make the most excellent of decisions and live life to the full. I know you are not a quitter. You are not. You are not. You are not a quitter. It is not normal for a born again to quit. It is unborn again! Get up! Talk to somebody today and join forces. But don't ever let quitting cross your mind. You do not know what quitting is and you are not about to find out, now or throughout eternity. Never. You are more than a conqueror.

6.

RIVALS FOREVER

Revelation 12:12b *Woe to the inhabiters of the earth and*
of the sea! For the devil is come down unto you,
having great wrath, because he
knoweth that he hath
but a short
time.

ANYONE can tell from the scripture above, the devil is not here on honeymoon. He is bitter. He is raving mad. **Not only is the time short for him, but he sees that man has been highly exalted and blessed.** There are many blessings we need to lay hold of and in the remaining chapters; we shall touch some of them. What is yours comes to you this very day in Jesus' name. How you behave after knowing something matters. You are no longer ignorant. This is the moment we begin the climax of Satan's best kept secrets. The real reasons he can never reconcile with you, the real reasons he can never love any human being, born again or not.

Bitterness as you read from the scripture is the basis for Satanism. He hates everyone. It does not matter whether you are in Satanism or not. He hates you. He can use you to further his program, but never will he come an inch closer to loving you. **He is bitter.** In fact, two factors play a role in those who get into his kingdom. **Bitterness and Selfishness.** The devil knows everyone who worships him does so because they are blinded by bitterness (Remember Simon in Acts 8?) or selfishness. Satanists are mostly people who have been deeply hurt in life. Bitterness fills their lives. Nothing makes sense. Some even contemplate suicide. Usually, a person who is ready to kill himself can easily kill someone else. It is in such moments when some recruiter points them to Satan as the solution. When the door has closed behind, they discover they were better off without the devil's goodies. The devil has this principle: **If someone joins you out of selfish ambition, you always watch that person carefully. In fact you put the 'fear of god' to keep him in check.** He keeps them under constant threats. The devil is **hardcore evil!** Unfortunately, the devil's evil has been so watered down that there are some who even sympathize with him.

Christ Jesus has made a provision when you become born again to lead a life different from others if only you cooperate with the Holy Spirit. Remember the Holy Spirit is here for you. He has no business here without you. John 14. He is here to teach you, guide you, comfort you etc. But the question that arises is this one: Is He doing any of these things in your life? If not, why? Now that you have realized that you are a new creation, let us touch on that a little further.

I. THE KINGDOMS

There are three kingdoms

- ✓ **The Kingdom Of God**

- ✓ **The Kingdom Of Man**

- ✓ **The Kingdom Of Satan**

These three kingdoms have two very unique principles or laws by which they operate.

- ✓ **The Law of the Blood**

- ✓ **The Law of the Word.**

1. **The Kingdom Of God–Matthew 6:33**

> Matthew 6:33 *But seek ye first **the kingdom of God**, and his righteousness; and all these*

things shall be added
unto you.

Appearing in the kingdom of God without being born into it is impossible. Unheard of. **You can never join God's Kingdom**. The only way of doing it is by being born into it! And it is impossible to be born into it without the shedding of **blood**. Everyone who is born from above is born by the blood of Jesus. Eph. 1:7 and

Heb. 9:11 But Christ being come an high priest of good things to come, by a greater and more perfect tabernacle, not made with hands, that is to say, not of this building; 12 Neither by the blood of goats and calves, but by his own blood he entered in once into the holy place, having obtained eternal redemption for us. 13 For if the blood of bulls and of goats, and the ashes of an heifer sprinkling the unclean, sanctifieth to the purifying of the flesh: 14 How much more shall the blood of Christ, who through the eternal Spirit offered himself without spot to God, purge your conscience from dead works to serve the living God?
15 And for this cause he is the mediator of the new testament, that by means of death, for the redemption of the transgressions that were under the first testament, they which are called might receive the promise of eternal inheritance. 16 For where a testament is, there must also of necessity be the death of the testator. 17 For a testament is of force after men are dead: otherwise it is of no strength at all while the testator liveth.

This blood that Jesus shed binds you eternally to the covenant God made. There is no covenant greater than a blood covenant. **Blood covenants vary in degrees of power.** The highest is the human sacrifice. But even this varies in power. The power depends on the purity of the human to be sacrificed. **The sacrifice of Jesus is the highest because He was the only pure human being. Before Him there was none, after Him, there is still nothing!** We shall touch on this in greater detail later. Jesus has given us life, and we shouldn't take it lightly. This gift of eternal life is free. You do not pay anything.

2. The Kingdom Of Man–Daniel 4:17

Daniel 4:17 *...the living may know that the*

> *most High ruleth in* **the**
> **kingdom of men**...

A person has only one channel of coming to earth. He or she must be born. If you were not born you aren't human.

> _{John 16:21} *"A woman, when she is in labor, has sorrow because*
> *her hour has come; but as soon as she has given birth*
> *to the child, she no longer remembers the*
> *anguish, for joy that a human*
> *being has been* **born into**
> **the world.**
> (Emphasis added)

The child only comes out when the mother has done her part of blood shedding too. No child is born without a drop of blood. Leviticus 12:4–7. Blood shedding is inevitable for someone to be born on earth. **You don't join the kingdom of men you are born into it.** And you do not pay anything. A person who is from the kingdom of man is referred to as **unspiritual** or **natural man.**

> _{1 Corinthians 2:14} *But the natural man does not receive*
> *the things of the Spirit of God, for they are*
> *foolishness to him; nor can he*
> *know them, because they are*
> *spiritually discerned.*
> (NKJV)

3. The Kingdom Of Satan–Matthew 12:26

> _{Matthew 12:26} *And if Satan cast out Satan, he is*
> *divided against himself; how shall then*
> **his kingdom** *stand?*
> (Emphasis added)

Against popular imagination, you don't join the devil's kingdom...you are born into it. Yes Satanists are 'born again' in some sense. Another 'born again'. The only thing that is unique about these births is that while you have no choice about being born in the second, you have a choice to be born in the first and third .i.e. from above—you become God's child or below—in the Satanic kingdom (*where the Antichrist emerges from*) you become Satan's child. In the devil's kingdom, you are born into it by the shedding of blood. It must first be your blood then that of others.

> Psalm 16:4 *Their sorrows shall be multiplied that hasten*
> *after another god:* **their drink offerings of blood**
> **will I not offer, nor take up their**
> *names into my lips*
> (Emphasis added)

The psalmist refuses to be 'born' into the devil's kingdom. There is a system of progression. First you are on lower levels. Playing or toying with various demonic items like charms. When this level is passed, you begin blood shedding. Simple things are killed, cats, dogs, chickens. But later when one wants to go deeper, for one reason or the other they offer their blood and the blood of other humans. Human sacrifice is regular or else your blood is the one requested.

> Hebrews 9:16 *For where a testament is, there must also of necessity*
> *be the death of the testator.* *17 For a testament is of*
> *force after men are dead: otherwise it is of*
> *no strength at all while the*
> *testator liveth.*

Human sacrifice is the highest sacrifice in the universe! Blood sacrifices are the key to unlocking spiritual power. Blood sacrifices open spiritual kingdoms. So, when satanists offer their blood sacrifices and pledge to offer more they have literally died! They are now born-again, not as the weak mortals they were before the ritual, but as immortals, gods! The more they kill people, offer blood sacrifices, the more they are elevated and given access to certain information and spiritual power!

Satanists are demonically born-again. But one could ask: Why all the constant sacrifices? While it is true their master is cruel and blood thirsty, there is one secret that all satanist are not told: **Only a perfect sacrifice stops the demand for further sacrifice.** Since a Satanist's blood is not holy or pure, and even that of his or her victims, further sacrifices will always be requested. Satanists must save themselves! *Believe in yourself.* Remember that expression? It has a different meaning. Not the way you take it dear. In the kingdom of Satan there is no universal sacrifice only personal sacrifice. It is demanded of individuals to perform or make way, by excruciating death!

> Psalm 16:4 ***Their sorrows shall be multiplied that hasten after another god****: their drink offerings of blood will I not offer, nor take up their names into my lips*
> (Emphasis added)

As already stated, when one is demonically born-again, they acquire names. Names of authority. That's what the Psalmist is saying in 16:4.

> Psalm 106:37 *They even sacrificed their sons And their daughters to demons,* [38] *And shed innocent blood, The blood of their sons and daughters, Whom they sacrificed to the idols of Canaan; And the land was polluted with blood.*
> (NLT)

The demon in charge of human sacrifice—Chemosh, demands nothing less than your beloved one. The dearer the person is to you, the more acceptable the sacrifice.

But it is important to note that it is only in the devil's kingdom that the one who wants to be born makes a personal sacrifice! He or she pays to be born into it. And he or she further makes more sacrifice to maintain the position. Satan is never sacrificial. This is not free as you can see. You work for it.

> Romans 6:23 *For the wages of sin is death; but*
> *the gift of God is eternal life*
> *through Jesus Christ*
> *our Lord.*

The wages of sin is death. A wage is a salary. You work for it. And you must expect a payment. For all the wickedness you are committing you will be rewarded. And your reward is justified. **God will destroy you and your god. Get ready.**

Christians and non–Christians have often asked why a loving God could create Hell for people. Good question, but a very wrong one. Hell is not for human beings. God has clearly said that hell is not for humans

> Matthew 25:41 *... into the everlasting fire*
> *prepared for the devil and*
> *his angels...*
> (NKJV)

But Pastor Keyworth, what do we say about those people who are going there?

Have you ever attended a meeting and found people who were not supposed to be there, in attendance? Good. Dear, those are what we call **Gatecrashers**. You must be a very determined gatecrasher to get to Hell. And I'm serious about this. Hell is personal preference.

II. THE KNIGHTS OF THE NIGHT

Dear friend this is the point when I bring you home. *Down to earth*. In both God's Kingdom and in Satan's Kingdom the people in them are not ordinary beings. **They are spirit beings**. While the earthly is natural the other two are supernatural. Are you ready for the reality check? That fella with a sweet smile at work, that fella you rub shoulders with could just be a spirit being from the kingdom of hell. '*Uh, now he is scaring instead of encouraging*'. It does not hurt to be informed, but to be uninformed is disastrous. Many are uncomfortable when someone tells them what is wrong. They want to be flattered. Flattery is the Antichrist's (PAD) personal assistant demon. Flattery is what the devil will use in the last days to scoop many out of eternal life if they are not careful. Of course, we know there are those whose calling is presentation of damaging facts. When they bring down someone that is when they feel anointed. I am not the sort. I believe in balanced Christianity.

Escape the snare of the enemy today. Be teachable. Christianity of ignorance is not Christianity. Others have suggested we move in love. Wonderful. Great. **Love at the expense of Jesus is not love but idolatry.** May I inform you that certain relationships must be severed for you to lead a victorious life. There is a big difference between wisdom and cowardice. Some 'wisdoms' must be checked. If a chicken is training a lion, that lion is finished. It will lose character. Friend you are entering a zone where it may just cost you dearly. *Honeymoon just flew out of the window.* That relationship you have with that person is not right, you know it. Cut it. I'm talking to you. What seems beneficial now may prove fatal to you later. **Blessed is the person who has cut evil ties.** Psalm 1:1–3. Some people have not known that their pastors, bishops even spouses are engaged in underworld activities. Friend I am opening your eyes. We should not live in suspicion, but live alert and be led by the Holy Spirit. Many are living in ignorance and cannot understand why they are victims. Associations. Our Lord told us to **'watch'** and pray. But like the great geniuses we are, we just pray. The devil has been asking his deputies this, 'Guys tell me am not dreaming.' And they respond, 'Your Wickedness, you ain't. They are blind and dumb!' With that he chuckles, gleefully.

For example, you have been experiencing strange afflictions, ask yourself questions. Today there is this disease upon you.

When you are prayed for, you seem to see healing. After a few days it has moved from the leg to the hand. Then the cycle continues. Perhaps it is business. Your business doesn't just seem to find its feet. But others are flourishing in theirs. We are in a no delimitation moment. There are no neutrals. The times we live in are no respecter of either your education or your position. You can have all the degrees and positions and still find life hard.

Frustrations here and there. Suicide starts even beckoning. **People have realized man cannot do without the spirit world. He will either lean on Satan or God. That is the world we live in today. Not believing in the Supernatural does not make you 'modern,' it makes you super ignorant and a victim.** Wake up. The most important degree to have is the spiritual degree. It is not gained from a college, but through a personal relationship with Jesus.

God, the Holy Spirit is ready to get you closer to Him. It is your only hope. A lot is going on. **Some things are done to fool you.** I wish you could understand. The world has a new religion. It is witchcraft. The intensity, the levels are abnormal. And Christians seem to be clueless. It is funny that the devil knows this message is true, but the believers do not know, what is right, wrong or what is in between, if there is such a thing. The devil has made profit. He is laughing all the way to the bank. While Christians move around hopelessly with their little carnal agendas, satanic strategies are being devised and implemented. Some men, clad in expensive suits, are in meetings discussing ways to convince the world why child molestation should be legalized. How could we be dumb, when people are planning to be putting their penises in babies' mouths for sexual pleasure and as an honour to their master? They will fight tooth and nail to have those rights legalized. **But we know what is legal before man is not always legal before God.** Pederasts come in many forms. And how honourable and angelic these devils appear! Yes Vince? What a dumb question Vince. Of course the baby will think the penis is a feeding bottle as it sucks!

How I desire you to understand that what we are talking about is what is happening around us right now. I have never been so appalled by the love for the demonic than what I have seen in my lifetime. And when you talk about it, *Hey Hush... That is segregative.* And when did the Gospel become all inclusive? The Holy Ghost and demons sharing a cup of coffee and muffins in the name of love? Give me a better joke.

I am not here to become popular. My lecturer once said, 'The same people praising you today are the same people crucifying you tomorrow'. How correct that man of God was. I do not need a name. I have one already. **JESUS**. It is Jesus and no other. As we associate let us mind certain wisdoms. **For there are many among us, who are the true enemies of the Lord Jesus**. I know this is the gospel the world is not ready for. Our children have a game they play, Hide and Seek. And they say, 'Ready or not, here I come'. Ready or not we deliver the Gospel at your door step. What you do with it is up to you.

It is appalling to see a false calculated **unity** enveloping us. In the name of Love and Oneness, we are even loving the devil and uniting with him. The devil cannot even believe it. The shock is too much. He now suffers from High Blood Pressure. But my standpoint is clear: **It is better for truth to divide us than for sin to unite us.**

I know this is your stance too. We must choose between the Fame and the Faith. And we choose the Faith.

Jesus gave me a **word** for someone who I knew was very stubborn. I refused to go there. I knew he would reject it. I told God, 'He won't accept it.'

It is better for truth
to divide us
than for sin to unite us

And I lay on my bed. Suddenly a hand pulled my spirit out of my body. And the Lord said, 'Don't you ever disobey me, whatever

I tell you to speak go and speak, whether they believe it or not.' That happened around 07:00 a.m. I was wide–awake. Then He released my spirit and it slumped back into my body. From that day, I do not carry out a referendum before I deliver God's Word. *Do not ask me if I went and delivered the message or not.*

Knowledge is power. But it depends on what kind of knowledge is before you. There is a great trick that Satan has been using repeatedly and many seem to stumble over it. Deception. True Perspective is vital in escaping this vice. The devil, you must know dear, has an army. This army unfortunately, comprises people. I know am treading on some dangerous theological grounds, allow me to explain, your majesty.

> Philippians 2:25 *Yet I supposed it necessary to send to you Epaphroditus, my* **brother**, *and companion in* **labour**, *and* **fellowsoldier**, *but your* **messenger**, *and he that* **minister**ed *to my wants.*
> (Emphasis added)

When we study the Bible properly, we get more clarity. And our lives make more sense. Who was Epaphroditus?

- ✓ He was a Brother,
- ✓ A Labourer,
- ✓ **A Soldier**,
- ✓ A Messenger and
- ✓ A Minister.

My point? Just as we are soldiers of Jesus, out there are soldiers of Satan. Believe it or not, cry or laugh that is the situation right now.

> Psalm 2:1 *Why do the heathen rage, and the people imagine*
> *a vain thing? ² The kings of the earth **set themselves**,*
> *and the rulers take counsel together, against the*
> *LORD, and against his anointed, saying, ³ Let*
> *us break their bands asunder, and cast*
> *away their cords from us.*
> (Emphasis added)

They have **set** themselves against the LORD. The word **set** means they have taken a position, a stance against the LORD. And the fact that they take their stance against the LORD means they are **spiritual people**. They know what God stands for and they do not want it. And if they are doing all this, they cannot be atheists. **Not everyone is doing things out of ignorance. Their ancestors the Pharisees did the same.** The resurrection of Jesus never moved them. It takes a hardened heart, to have all the proof before him and still opt for ways to cause unbelief. The Pharisees were the first to put their accounts to satanic use, to block the Gospel of Jesus. If their descendants do the same today, should that surprise us? *The apple doesn't fall further from the?* Good answer, Toni. *From the Pharisees.* There are so many spiritual people in our midst. The Apostle Paul called them the enemies of the cross. And these people live among us. Understand that only a spiritual person will decide the course this world has to take. So, **if** what you have just read is **really true**, some people are not ordinary, then you are **unprotected!** Those people can turn your life upside down until life becomes meaningless. Most of them **their mission** is to force you through unfortunate happenings, **to seek counsel** or help from them. Then the door locks behind you and another unsuspecting victim is ushered into eternal oblivion. Satanism is a one way street. They don't want you coming out. Why? You have known their deception, they don't want you to inform the sleeping masses. **Not everyone you meet is ordinary.** They have been to places that can make every hair on that body stand on its end. Those people you cross paths with are high–ranking officials in the spirit. This is one of the devil's key effective strategies; **Hit you from an angle you do**

not anticipate. Write this in your heart: **Not every friendly person in your life is your friend.** *But Pastor Keyworth they give me gifts!* **My dear novice, ever heard of** *'bait'?*

Let me tell you this. If you are born again, it is time to comprehend you are not simple. You are supernatural. The power you have to effect changes around you is more than the devil's. The secret of making it in Christian maturity is having a 'Holy Ghost Stubborn Faith'. I remember my pastor called me and said, 'Keyworth, you are stubborn, but it is good stubbornness!' Have a faith that never says, 'No'. Once on the move it does not look back. The Bible says you cannot separate a fool from his folly even if you pound him in a mortar with a pestle. Well, that is where we Christians have something in common with fools. We ain't quitters. It is in our being. Our nature. Somebody once said we have no reverse gear!! I agree. Not even death can stop me. I don't fear it and the first witness I can call upon is the devil himself! Satan knows Keyworth does not fear him and Keyworth does not fear death. On that we don't even argue, it is settled! I have told the devil **repeatedly**, 'Look into my eyes. If you see **any trace** of fear, I will fall down and worship you.' *He has constant diarrhea.* I have always said this and I'll repeat it. **The devil only respects those who oppose him not those who serve him**. Someone said, 'Pastor but cowards live long'. No they don't. They have no life of their own to start with... They live in torment all their lives and serve that which they loath! They laugh not when they want to, but when someone wants them to. Every time they expect disaster. They live in fear. What a life! It is inhuman, no wonder even the reward is inhuman—the flames

Revelation 21:8 *But the cowardly, the unbelieving, the vile, the murderers, the sexually immoral, those who practice magic arts, the idolaters and all liars—their place will be in the fiery lake of burning sulfur. This is the second death."* (Emphasis added)

The only way to stop being a victim is either to go to the devil's camp and surrender or become born again in Jesus' Kingdom... When you become born again friend you are not ordinary. To be born again in God's Kingdom and still be ordinary is a sin. The Bible states that there are two kinds of sins. The sin of commission—wrong things done and the sin of omission—right things not done (neglected).

Let us address something here. Do you want to be born again? Say this prayer and mean every letter in it. You are not parroting it. Talk to God. Your faith must be in the saving power of Jesus the Son of God and not in the prayer. He has your attention. Heaven is still, it is silent. That is how important this is.

PRAYER

*God I believe Jesus is not a story,
He is real. He came on earth, He
died that I might live. I believe He
died and rose from the dead by the
power of the Holy Spirit.
Jesus with my heart, my mind, my
mouth and everything in me I
confess you as my Lord and Savior.
Your blood was shed on the cross
for all my sins to be washed away.
I believe they are gone.
I ask you to come and live in me now.
I believe that by faith Jesus you
live in me. You are welcome. I'll live for
you now. Thank you I believe I am
now born again. Amen.*

My dear the devil has no power over you now. Colossians 1:12–13. Heaven is full of noise now. Fireworks are going off! Serious music is being played for you.

Luke 15:10 *Likewise, I say unto you, there is joy in the presence of the angels of God over one sinner that repenteth.*

Welcome home. Now you can call God your Father, before this He never recognized you as His child. Friend that is the beginning, go forward. Read the Bible and just like the way you prayed in faith, you can continue praying and believing He hears you in your other requests. Pray every day. Talk to God. Tell Him everything, do not be shy. Let Him guide you, and advise you. Simply ask in prayer. Can you please God? Yes. Just believe what He says. All these things that seem strange will become reality.

Now get this. These two kingdoms, the first and the third determine what happens on earth. Satan has sent his own to control the earth and God has sent his own. The ones sent by God are officially recognized as ambassadors, 2 Corinthians 5:19. The devil does not argue about that. As an ambassador, the place where you are belongs to your government. It is holy property. Satan keeps off! If you don't believe this you are doomed. God knows you as an ambassador. Angels see you that way, demons see you that way, but how do you see yourself?

One should know though, that, there is something about the word 'ambassador'. It seems to suggest that only a mature Christian is actually an ambassador. **A person who is dedicated to spiritual growth.** Maturity is simply more of the Word actively in you. If the Word is dormant in you, you are not mature. Grow in the grace God has given. Keep on growing.

Pastors, preachers whatever you call them, have for years and years echoed what the Bible says: **To anyone who believes there is nothing impossible.** That means you. And with God nothing is impossible. **These two persons have no enough challenges to stop them. The good news is that they are on the same team.** Friend, learn to meditate on God's Word. Why are we putting emphasis on the Word? **All these kingdoms are controlled by words. This is the second principle by which these kingdoms operate.** So, ambassador, live by the word. Know that maturity is realizing your life is supernatural. Things around you are being influenced by some 'strange' supernatural factors it's time to put your foot down. Get up lazy corporal. March forward. Every confession you make empowers you. Every. **You don't have to feel it has happened. You know it has.** By the way that is also a sign of maturity. Ambassador there is no setback for you. Everything works out for good. Romans 8:28. This scripture is best understood when you look at Satan's stronghold death and how God used that very **ace** in the devil's claw to mangle Satan on his home ground. God is all-knowing He cannot be outwitted. His dynasty rules. Ambassador you are not here for games. This is serious business.

People have this idea that Satan owns the world and Christians are in the fringes somewhere, on the outskirts trying to survive on a drop of water per day. That is demonic. **There is no biblical basis for saying the devil is the master of this world anymore! There is no scripture that backs this. Yes even with all the satanic strategies in place, and well implemented, the devil is not in charge. Even when the Antichrist heads the one world government the devil is not in charge! Jump out of folklore!**

Jesus has all power and authority He is in charge, because He is the ONLY King of kings and Lord of lords! And the good news is, we His disciples must exercise that now! Why? There is going to be a power transfer. There have been a lot of transfers you have not been aware of. You will pinch yourself for refusing to know this. The devil hates you with all of his being because of what God has done—stripping him of everything and giving and lumping it all on you!!! *Oh God, you didn't get it.* This bloke you call the devil is stripped, stranded and left to dry.

> There is no biblical basis for saying the devil is the master of this world anymore!

^{Psalm 68:19} *Blessed be the Lord, who daily*
loadeth us with benefits, even
the God of our
salvation.

Let us look closely at just six of the benefits that have made the devil mad. And the devil does not want you to know this. If you know, you will see him as he really is, stripped to the bone!

III. THE KINGLY BLESSINGS

1. ABODE: EDEN

Adam's Eden is not the first Eden. It is quite evident from the scriptures that there have been two Edens. The first, Lucifer was in charge of, the second Adam was. Lucifer's Eden preceded Adam's. Lucifer's Eden is found in

^{Ezekiel 28:13} *You were in Eden, the garden of God; every precious*
stone adorned you: ruby, topaz and emerald, chrysolite, onyx
and jasper, sapphire, turquoise and beryl. Your settings and
mountings were made of gold; on the day you were
*created they were prepared.*¹⁴ *You were anointed*
as a guardian cherub, for so I ordained
you. You were on the holy mount of God; you walked
*among the fiery stones.*¹⁵ *You were blameless*
in your ways from the day you were
created till wickedness was
found in you.

Adam's is in Genesis. God gave Eden to Adam and Satan could just watch from a distance. He must have thought he was having one of those crazy nightmares. Unfortunately, this was real life. Jealous was very much at play when the devil tempted Adam. The devil is jealousy even today. First, understand what jealous is.

A. JEALOUS

Jealous is conceding your inferiority. **Only the inferior are jealousy of others.** The superior are never jealousy of anyone. Why would they be? **Superiority is a spiritual and not a social position.** King Saul had limousines and great designer suits from France and Italy, but that never stopped him from unleashing the Secret Service on David, a harpist and small-scale farmer. Whenever the king looked at David, he was convinced David was superior. **The Inferior have a personal conviction that they are inferior.** Did David say he was superior? No. But at the mention of the name of David, the Great President Saul Kish went into serious convulsions! Even when David's music couldn't sell on the market, his excellency was convinced it could top the world charts! When he heard his wives talk good of David, he concluded, in a hoarse and threatening voice, 'You want to go to bed with him, huh?' *Come on Saul, you are losing it.* Never live in jealous friend, you are not inferior.

Jealousy is the ultimate acceptance that one is a failure through and through and that nothing will change, hence the jealous. It is the devil's character. It is demotion. **The devil has conceded he is a total failure and things will never change, that's why he hates all human beings.** And this is the reason he turns people on people so that they destroy one another. He wants to see all of them destroyed. Seriously speaking, there is no one who is the devil's beloved. All are victims in his wicked claws. He wants nothing but pain in the lake of fire for the most obedient and most hard working Satan worshiper. Nothing else. **He has taught them deception. But what they fail to see is that in the same way he tells them to lie and use deceit on others, he is using the same lies and deceit on them!** *You don't have to be a kindergarten dropout to know that.* Lying and being lied to. Deceiving and being deceived. 2 Timothy 3:13. This is a great secret he keeps. Most of his followers do not know this. But when they do, in the lake of fire, I am sure they will gang up on the devil and beat the devil out of him. Better get good doctors in there fast. That scripture is from the KNV—Keyworth Ngosa Version. But there is something close to that.

> Isaiah 14:10 *All they shall speak and say unto thee,*
> *Art thou also become weak as we? Art*
> *thou become like unto us?*

Tempers will flare-up in the Lake of Fire. There will be a terrible stushie that I fear for the devil and his demons! Hardcore murderers will be there don't forget. So don't rule out the devil being murdered! (Please don't quote me on that!) Human beings have the potential to 'ascend' to where God has destined them to be—God's Throne, the very thing the devil wanted! But the devil doesn't have such a chance!

> Revelations 3:21 *To him that overcometh will I grant*
> *to sit with me in my throne, even as I*
> *also overcame, and am set down*
> *with my Father in*
> *his throne.*

Don't forget that. See Isaiah 14:12–14. And what the devil fails to mention is that he has been judged and his sentence already given. But all those humans he has working under him are not. They have the potential to leave and that is why he must demand hardcore wickedness from them. He is constantly trying to corrupt them further and make them as guilty as he is before God, Jehovah.

> John 16:11 *Of judgment, because the*
> *prince of this world*
> *is judged.*

One of the elementary principles of judgement is that the one who is being judged is inferior to the judgement seat he stands before. Since the devil stood before God's judgement seat, he is inferior. All his superiority he tries to display are mere antics of a pretender. The future of a guilty person is in the hands of the judge! And in judgement only the truth is sought, not lies. This is the folly of all who follow the devil. No lie can save you that day. None.

1Corinthians 6:2 *Do ye not know that the saints shall judge the world? and if the world shall be judged by you, are ye unworthy to judge the smallest matters?*

The Bible is sweet!!! Terry you are a judge! Congratulations. Yes Judge Jane. You are a qualified judge! As long as you are a saint, you qualify. Who is a saint? One who is born-again. Not the quickie born-again. The true born-again. May God have mercy on those who will be judged by Sr. Mary. She has a temper which even the devil dreads. Friend the wicked should not move you because you are still meeting. In your court! Imagine driving to court. On the way someone rams into your car. He insults and punches you. He flees before you could even get his vehicle's registration number. What is disturbing is that in all that you did him no wrong. But by some sweet twist of life, you cross paths again. Only that this time, you are the judge presiding over his first degree murder case. And he can't change judges. Before you even study the case, you know the character of the defendant! Are you going to smile and give him a place in the sun? **Never!**

Friend the wicked should not move you because you are still meeting. In your court!

Believe me, somehow somewhere there will be enough liquid to create a lake from those pants of his! When your eyes lock and he slowly recognizes you, he knows and you know, he's a goner! This is the situation we are facing. Let them jump now. I hope you will never forget this secret. The world is coming to be judged, by you!!! I think that calls for dancing. Put the book down and dance my lord Judge.............. (your name)

Brethren, let me quickly point out that there is a very important point the Bible mentions in verse 14 of Ezekiel 28, this anointed cherub was **walking in the midst of the stones of fire.** A closer look at the **stones of fire** reveals some interesting gems. It was at this moment that this cherub *seems* to have been entrusted with being the leader among those seraphims of fire or **gifted builders or masons**! The gift of masonry he came with it, when he fell. Though perverted now, the gift is still at work. Believe it or not he is an **architect.** It sounds weird, but it is very true. And when he fell, he came with this gift. When they call him GAOTU, Great Architect Of The Universe—they are mesmerized at the gift he has. The devil has plotted the world system in a strange way. It is an intricate web of death. The way he span democracy, communism, etc and the confusions he raises by pitting one group against another is classic genius. Evil genius though. The way he has woven and taken over the Church where people at the bottom know they have different denominations that can never even by a strange miracle, see eye to eye, when in fact it is one thing at the top, is mesmerizing. The way he has span alternatives to holy living is shocking. The solutions he has offered the world is beyond stupendous. But **a gift**, though perverted, this skill remains. What his worshippers forget to grasp though, is this, **IT IS A GIFT**. And if it is a gift, there is the giver. And the giver is always greater than the recipient.

> Hebrews 7:7 *And without doubt the lesser person is blessed by the greater.* (NIV)

Could Ezekiel 28:14 be the origin of Satan's title of Lord of the fire, which has chameleoned into 'V' hand gestures today? Is it really true the 'V' salute means victory? YES! It is both a war cry and a form of worship. It is a war cry to keep on fighting till victory is gained over all that belongs to Jesus Christ. Psalm 2. It is also the rejection of Jesus' peace and embracing of Satan's peace. Our educated, yet unwise populace flashes this symbol without an iota of understanding! *Educated illiterates!* Their 'peace' is actually freedom from anything that stands for Jesus the Christ. So when one gestures, one is really saying Satan is going to finally win and give us the 'peace' we desire. When you look at this 'V' gesture from the Cabala, it becomes even clearer; the majority are worshipping Satan unknowingly. We save the gruesome details for another day.

2. ANOINTED CHERUB THAT COVERS

A grade above the rest, but that is as far as a creature could go in being close to God. Ezekiel 28:14, Exodus 25:19–20. But with man God takes inconceivable strides of elevating him. Man does not cover the throne he sits in the throne! Revelation 3:21. The very thing Satan ogled at and craved for until his eyeballs became sore is yours. *How d'you expect the devil to love you?*

By virtue of being born human, even if you are in Satanism, the devil knows the potential you have of becoming his boss. The devil does not hate some humans, **he hates All Humans**. The sooner you realize this, the better. That is why he keeps his servants in death threats. **The devil doesn't only destroy outsiders, he destroys even his own.** No one is spared! No one. He uses some people to destroy others, by giving them power. The devil's power is always for stealing, killing or destroying and nothing else. *Talk about enlightenment!* The real reason is to make them as guilty as he is! The whole idea is to make you guilty. The question of eternity is, guilty before who? Bobo, the devil is jealous of you. It must not be a secret anymore.

Ephesians 2:6 *And God raised us up with Christ and seated us with him in the heavenly realms in Christ Jesus,* 1:20b *....and seated him at his right hand in the heavenly realms,* 21 *far above all rule and authority, power and dominion, and every title that can be given, not*

only in the present age but
also in the one
to come.

In rank, right now we are far superior to him. You, believe it or not, are above any title that has been, that is and that will be. This means that as a Christian you will always be superior to the devil forever and ever. This is not good news to the devil. **He hates you because you are his Boss.** There is more.

3. BEAUTY: CLOTHING

According to the Bible no creature was ever clothed like him. In the devil's knowledge, God couldn't do anything beyond. Well, he goofed himself all the way to Hell.

> Ezekiel 28:13 *You were in Eden, the garden of God; every precious stone adorned you: ruby, topaz and emerald, chrysolite, onyx and jasper, sapphire, turquoise and beryl. Your settings and mountings were made of gold; on the day you were created they were prepared.¹⁴ You were anointed as a guardian cherub, for so I ordained you. You were on the holy mount of God; you walked among the fiery stones.¹⁵ You were blameless in your ways from the day you were created till wickedness was found in you.*

As for man it's extremely unique. We are clothed with Christ. Romans 13:14, Galatians 3:27. The word 'beautiful' falls short of describing a zillionth of how splendid you are in Christ! **There is no beauty like God's beauty!!** Many a child of God has been convinced by an ugly devil that they are ugly. The devil is a comedian. When the devil comes and talks about beauty, laugh at him. I'm serious. Laugh at him until he cries. He is ugly. Demons are ugly. I know what I have encountered. A natural man, from the kingdom of man, cannot look at the devil without collapsing (fainting) just because of his **ugliness!** And I mean that in a literal sense. Beauty is only in God's presence. And this is the fella who comes to try and depress you that you are ugly? Tell the devil to buy a mirror! He will delete you from his mail list and he will never send you another email of depression.

4. BRILLIANT: WISDOM

As a unique being, God created him with special Wisdom. No creature had such wisdom. Lucifer felt untouchable. He magnified the gift more than the Giver. He insulted the wisdom of his maker and felt he could outwit Him. Ezekiel 28:12b. Friend, do you know that you are a genius? I mean that literally. Look at this

1 Corinthians 2:16b *... we have the mind of Christ.*

Nobody is as wise as you are child of God. It is impossible for a person who is born again to be dull. That would be a first. A miracle! You have the most advanced mind in the universe. Even Solomon in his best days does not come close to your level of wisdom. **Christ's mind is the most powerful mind to have ever existed on this planet, and that record is not going to be broken.** The good news is, you have it! Put the book down and stretch your legs, move around. Think about this. You are the wisest person on earth right now. *But Pastor Keyworth, I don't feel like that.* Good. I know. *But why?* You are still a baby. You don't know how to think. It's time you did. Throw the diapers child. God clearly says He wants to display His **Manifold** Wisdom to all the spiritual forces in the universe! And He is not using anyone daft. I have never met a Christian who is dull, though many are trying very hard in that department. I hope they don't succeed. **Breaking News: You are the instrument God is using to show His manifold wisdom. Ephesians 3:10.** The devil thought he had known all of God. That is the problem of familiarity.

But familiarity does not come alone. It tows along its cousin, humiliation! The cousin of familiarity is humiliation. Pride comes just before a mighty plunge downhill.

5. CONDUCTOR: PRAISE LEADER

According to Ezekiel 28:13b and Isaiah 14:11 Lucifer seems to have had a unique role in leading Praise and Worship in Heaven, before man existed. After his fall, God has switched things. He fired Lucifer (now devil) and guess who he has endorsed? You!

Psalm 22:3 *But thou art holy, O thou that inhabitest the praises of Israel.*

God has declared when man praises me **My glory comes down.** It manifests.

Psalm 149:3 *Let them praise his name in the dance: let them sing praises unto him with the timbrel and harp. ⁴ For the LORD taketh pleasure in his people: he will beautify the meek with salvation. ⁵ Let the saints be joyful in glory: let them sing aloud upon their beds.*

However, you don't do it to get something from God. It's part of you. Praise Him for who He is.

Psalm 145:3 *Great is the LORD, and greatly to be praised; and his greatness is unsearchable.*

Ever seen someone praising God when things were bad? They have a revelation. Praise always spits in the face of the situation. It doesn't count the challenge. Praise sees the outcome. Praise always has it, even though it seems not to have materialized! That gives the devil fits. When you have insight, you have insight.

Nothing can take it away from you, not even a situation. **The God we serve can never be out smarted.** That calls for praise even in the midst of storms. Praise is a diktat, a decree, an order.

And note that you don't have to be born again to praise Him. I have no headache over someone who is not born again praising God the Father or Jesus. **In fact you don't have to be human to praise Him.** You just have to be God's creation. It is mandatory. Period.

> Psalm 148:2 *Praise him, all his angels, praise him, all his heavenly hosts.³ Praise him, sun and moon, praise him, all you shining stars.⁴ Praise him, you highest heavens and you waters above the skies. ⁵ Let them praise the name of the LORD, for he commanded they were created.* (NIV)

Picture this assembly that gathers every day to give Him praise. Did you add your voice to the assembly today? If you didn't praise Him today, others did. Is there a difference between one who is born again and one who isn't as they praise God? Very much. To a child of God praise is not something you do. It is your dress code. It is a garment. It comes with the package when you are born again. This is the essence of this book. To know what is really yours. Isaiah 61:3. Praise is the nature of your spirit. You were created to praise Him, Isaiah 43:21

6. CROWN: LUCIFER

As could be seen from the scriptures, **'Lucifer' is actually an Office or title and not a personal name of a being.** Before the fall, this beautiful angelic being was called Lucifer. Let us look at one scripture from (KJV) and from NIV.

> Isaiah 14:12a *How art thou fallen from heaven, O Lucifer, son of the morning!*

Isaiah 14:12a *How you have fallen from heaven, O morning star, son of the dawn!*
(NIV)

Have you seen it? **Lucifer means Morning Star**, a title he tries to cling to up to this day. The Bible clearly states this has changed.

Revelation 22:16 *"I, Jesus, have sent my angel to give you this testimony for the churches. I am the Root and the Offspring of David, and the bright Morning Star."*
(NIV)

Okay, Church listen to this testimony: **Jesus is the Bright Morning Star!** Jesus wants the Church to know that when He got the Authority for heaven and earth He never left Satan anything! **He clearly got even the title of Morning Star.** The title that this angelic being held is no longer his. Jesus has taken everything the devil boasted about. **Satan has nothing**. The Bible says he is a Fugitive on earth! .

Revelation 2:26 *To him who overcomes and does my will to the end, I will give authority over the nations —²⁷ 'He will rule them with an iron scepter; he will dash them to pieces like pottery'— just as I have received authority from my Father.*

More bad news for Satan. **The nations he wanted so much to rule are all yours for free.** Reason number 7 for hating you. I know you missed that. People are killing others to be in power. . And you my beloved are just snoring and the nations are yours to rule because you are a Christian? Yep! Amazing.

1Corinthians 3:21 *Therefore let no man glory in men. **For***

> ***all things are yours;*** *²² Whether Paul, or Apollos,*
> *or Cephas,* ***or the world,*** *or life, or death, or*
> ***things present,*** *or* ***things to***
> ***come; all are yours...***
> (Emphasis added)

Listen, I am not proud, I am just in charge. Is the devil Jehovah's child? No. Then he is not a partaker of the blessing. Therefore he can never be the owner. The devil is not in charge! Let's finish with point number 6.

Beloved, Jesus is not interested in 'Lucifer'. He has a name higher than any other. What does he do with this prize? He makes it the children's bread.

> Revelation 2:26 *And he that overcometh, and keepeth my works unto the end, to him*
> *will I give power over the nations:* ²⁷ *And he shall*
> *rule them with a rod of iron; as the vessels of a potter*
> *shall they be broken to shivers: even as I received*
> *of my Father.* ²⁸ *And I will give him*
> *the morning star.*

Jesus is giving you the title or position of **The Morning Star.** It is finished for the devil, the secret is out. Now you know. The devil just wetted his pants. *I understand, some things shouldn't come out in the open.* The 'him' mentioned in the scripture is you. No... no... no Karen, it is not for men only, who bewitched you to think like that? In Christ, there is neither male nor female, Zambian nor American, Japanese nor Korean, Arab nor Jew. All are one. So the title of Morning Star is all yours for free. When the devil looks at you what does he see?

> 2 Peter 1:19 *And we have the word of the prophets made more certain, and you will*
> *do well to pay attention to it, as to a light shining*
> *in a dark place, until the day dawns and the*
> *morning star rises in your hearts.*
> (Emphasis added)

2 Corinthians 3:18 *And we, who with unveiled faces all reflect the Lord's glory, are being transformed into his likeness with ever-increasing glory, which comes from the Lord, who is the Spirit.* (NIV)

We are not only reflecting we are becoming more and more like Him, our Morning Star. This is what the Bible says in

Proverbs 4:18 *The path of the righteous is like the first gleam of dawn, shining ever brighter till the full light of day.* (NIV)

Keep in mind that the word 'path' means 'life'.

The LIFE of the righteous is like the first gleam of dawn, shining ever brighter till the full light of day.
(Paraphrased)

And check this

Ephesians 4:15 *But speaking the truth in love, may grow up into him in all things, which is the head, even Christ*
(Emphasis added)

The scripture is very clear, we are not growing up **IN** Him, we are growing up **INTO** Him! We are becoming more and more Him our Lord and Saviour. Look at this

Ephesians 5:30 *For we are members of his body, of his flesh, and of his bones.*

145

As a Christian, the intensity of your closeness to Christ is as a man and his body. In fact as a member of his body you and him are one. For Christ is the head and you are a member of his body... meaning you form one person! This closeness is shocking to comprehend, but truly it is so. Friend as we go to heaven we are going as Christ! That is the purpose for our growing INTO Him. But the opposite is frightening. Please understand this carefully. Don't mess it up with the New Age teachings.

Christ's rejection is becoming more and more serious. The rate is beyond appalling. What is happening to you dear is not something strange. Those who reject Jesus are becoming more intense in their wickedness. **It is clear from the Bible Romans 6:6 that sin is not what man does, but actually what he is!** Unrighteousness is a nature or character, it is what one is. So when you fully understand the purpose of the mark of the beast, to turn one into complete union with Satan, you realize people are going to hell not as sinners, but as the devil himself! I talk about this more in The Mystery Of Lawlessness. Righteousness is who you are. And us who have the glory of God are becoming more and more intense in reflecting His glory, for His mark, The Holy Spirit is here to turn us into Christ's very nature, His very image, so that we are like Christ. And the wicked? They are becoming fulltime devils!

> 1John 4:17 *Herein is our love made perfect, that we*
> *may have boldness in the day of judgment:*
> *because **as he is, so are we***
> *in this world.*
> (Emphasis added)

Timmy, you are reflecting Royalty. And there is no royalty without Authority. **The more you shine the more Satan sees the Morning Star arising in you**. Let me warn you. He is going to persecute you for it. The greatest danger the world faces today is not terrorism. No, no, no! The greatest danger the world faces is Christianity—the true Christianity. Every true Christian, is a danger to this world. And the devil and his family will do all they can to get rid of you. The reasons are evident, anyway. We can see through the god of this world system and we have refused to bow to something lower than us. Our loyalty is to the true King, Jesus. The devil is stranded and soon his time will be up, he shouldn't carry warm clothing to the lake of fire. Payday is just round the corner.

Does the devil still want to play chess with God? The last time I saw him he was being wheeled to a side ward, suffering from dangerous ulcers. He cannot sleep. Are you worried about something? Stop it. Just check out the devil. **Now that is what is called worrying.** The devil is the master of worrying. He is a commercial worrier! God has made 'Lucifer' an ordinary Title or position. There is no 'awe' in it. What Lucifer considered a special privilege for a selected few is now found in every common person's house. **God has spat on Satan's pride!**

Even in the world scenario, we know political leaders are a notch above the masses. Suppose by some twist all the privileges of presidents—great suits, expensive vehicles, great attention etc these things were now found even in the poorest of slums, would the president feel any more special? No? Why? Everything about him is now ordinary. Would you admire to be like him? Not in the next ten millenniums. Remember that God has not just stripped Satan and given you his position. He has loaded you with much more. The Holy Spirit will help you get these things. **God has loaded you with abnormal loads of blessings and you are about to discover the ultimate!**

7.

ENTHRONED: NO MORE BABES

1 Corinthians 3:1 *Brothers, I could not address you as spiritual but as worldly—mere infants in Christ.* (Emphasis added)

A casual glance gives us the impression Paul is talking about babe Christians. However, the opposite is the truth. He is talking about people that have refused to grow and he calls them 'not spiritual but still worldly'. These people could not take in mature teaching, all they wanted were basics. They are always learning spiritual preschool. A child who is at preschool for 30 years has a big problem. To accomplish what others achieve in a few years he must break Methuselah's age record! The Apostle Paul called these people worldly or carnal. Carnality is an archenemy of God. Mere infants are people who cannot confess the Word in Christ. They do not have the Christian language in them. They talk the world though they are Christians. They still do not know how God has stripped the devil and blessed them. They are being tossed back and forth because they are infants. Such babes are under a fugitive, Satan. They are imprisoned kings.

Babes of this sort are people who are not really committed to Christian growth. These are 'associate Christians'. **They are 'Christians' by virtue of coming to church, and not being born into the Kingdom.** They have a coat of religion, but far from seriousness. As long as the Word is caged in their mouth and it is not coming out, they are in trouble. The Bible equates the suppressing or enslaving 'elements' with 'gods' in Galatians 4 verses 8 and 9. All demonic gods that have enslaved people should never come near you. Satan and his cohorts should never make a slave out of you. It is impossible. Satan has jurisdiction just over his kingdom, but you are not in his kingdom. So how can he enslave you? Unless you make yourself 'not spiritual but worldly, a mere infant'.

> Colossians 1:13 *For he has rescued us from the*
> *dominion of darkness and brought us*
> *into the kingdom of the*
> *Son he loves...*
> (NIV)

Today all the devil's lies about you are diminishing. You must know who you are and whose you are. 'Lucifer' had his day now it is your day. No more being a babe. It is time to delve into the Word and progress in your walk with God. Refuse the status quo. Desire real growth in your walk with God.

> Ephesians 1:2 *Grace and peace to you from*
> *God our Father and the Lord*
> *Jesus Christ.* (NIV)

God the Father and the Lord Jesus give you grace freely. It says: Grace to you ....(put your name and speak it audibly) and peace...Now listen with your spirit. Grace is not just the name of a beautiful woman. Some people that is all they know. *Now you know why that guy is always saying, 'God give me Grace. God give me Grace.' He means the sister in the choir!* There is more to it than beautiful Grace. **Grace means three things**.

- ✓ **'Grace is <u>evident divine force</u> (ability) upon an <u>individual</u>.'** Grace is visible. It can be seen, it is experienced. People will see it when it is on you. Acts 11: 22–23. Joseph or Joses popularly known as Barnabas saw it. It is also upon you. **There is a blessing upon you to achieve anything!** The devil would want you to believe there is a curse for you to fail. No, dear. If you can remember this, the devil will stop laughing at you. **God has given us everything that pertains to this life and unto godliness.**

✓ **Grace is also favor.** 2 Corinthians 5:18 says we have been given the ministry of reconciliation. What does **Ministry of Reconciliation** really mean? It is simply **Restoration to Divine Favor!** You have been called to favor. The most important thing to realize is that God's favor upon you is for **life**.

> Psalm 30:5b *...his favor lasts a lifetime...* (NIV)

Can you tell how long that is? *Till you die*. Clap for yourself for giving the wrong answer. Death has no hold over you anymore! God's grace to you is unending. You have eternal life in you. Don't forget your nature. Why do you forget who you are? Confession... confession. **If there's an area where Satan has trapped God's children it's confession.** Do not speak demonic language. Speak words of life. God has favored you. **What do you call a person who is always favored by his boss or manager?** Correct. The boss' favorite. I remember a discussion I had with some friends.

One of them said, 'You Christians are fake. I know of some fake Christians, that's why I can't be a Christian.'

I have heard of that lame duck excuse before. I am sure you have too.

I said, 'But why do you look to the fake not the true Christians, why go for the worst grade out of the lot?'

His friends chipped in.

They said, 'We have a problem, can your God change the situation? We need three miracles to change everything.'

I said, 'The God I worship is not limited, that is nothing to Him.'

When I said that one of them became offended and said, 'The problem with you is that you think you are the only one who knows God.'

I said, 'I do not know about that, but what I do know is that I am God's favorite. From today start counting, your miracles are coming. I am going to pray.' To cut the short story shorter, the three miracles they requested came in a space of one month!

Child of God you are God's favorite. You are His best. Never be intimidated by a situation. God has favored you. You are God's favorite! A favored person is the favorite. (*That word just went through one ear out the other*). **When you are favored, you are favored.** Favor from your Father in heaven and the Lord Jesus is like Joseph's coat of many colors. It means you are daddy's 'spoilt' kid. **Your heavenly Father wants to 'spoil' you.** Have you ever seen spoilt kids before? They cry for this, the father provides. They cry for that the father provides. And I like the way the kids change their mouths and faces. **But there is one spoilt kid I have seen in the Bible—Jesus. He always got what He asked for.** John 11:42a. The only time He seemed not to get what He wanted was in Gethsemane, when He sweated drops of blood— an unusual occurrence called **Hematidrosis**, but even then, the Father's desire was so He could lavish Him with more goodies. Many people are mistaken. They think Jesus was afraid of death. Death could not hold Him. As a prophet He knew it. He foretold His rising from the dead. That was nothing. It didn't bother Him, that's why He told Peter to put away his little knife when he tried to defend Him. **Jesus did not want separation from the Father**). Today He is on the Right Hand of the Father. And what is on the Right Hand of the Father? Unending pleasures.

✓ **Pleasure is the third meaning of grace.**

Psalm 16:11 *Thou wilt show me the path of life: in thy presence is fulness of joy; at thy right hand there are pleasures for evermore.*

Do you know that from the day you got born-again God has used every excuse, some extremely flimsy, just to bless you more? That is why He loads you with blessings every day. Cooperate with Him so that there is that flimsy excuse. God's goodness is never-ending. **Do you know that there is a river of pleasures flowing right now?**

Pastor Keyworth, a river?

Yes. Some people the only river they know is the Zambezi. Dear Michael, there is something above the Zambezi River. The question is, are you drinking from it?

Psalm 36:7 *How excellent is thy lovingkindness, O God! therefore the children of men put their trust under the shadow of thy wings. 8 They shall be abundantly satisfied with the fatness of thy house; and thou shalt make them drink of the river of thy pleasures.*

Think about it. God does not stop on grace. It includes peace. **Peace is not just rest. It is rest plus prosperity.** Oh I know that is a misused word. But if God says it, so it is. The devil has used a reverse strategy. He lets some of his yoyos run around and talk so much prosperity, to the point that many of God's people are ready to embrace poverty for a change. I'm aware of prosperity for the sake of prosperity. There is no careless prosperity in Christianity. Try next door. **Many when they see Jesus is not dancing to their incessant childish tunes they flee to Gad and Meni, the demons of 'Good luck, fortune (*I can assure you it is misfortune*) and Gambling. Isaiah 65:11.** Do not fall for a lie. What is the Bible saying then about Grace? Read it aloud. *The evident divine ability upon me (in all I do) rest and prosperity from God My Daddy and the Master of the Universe Jesus (who is My Brother) is mine for free.* Is God the Father, Daddy? Don't ask me ask the Bible.

Romans 8:15 *And by him we cry,*
"Abba, Father."
(NIV)

The word for 'Abba' is not mere distant 'father' but one, which means 'Papa' or 'Daddy'. I know some of you have lived in boot camps. The picture you have of a father brings nothing less than hell. Beatings, sexual and verbal abuse all evils that could be done, your father has bettered the record. You believe your father is approaching devil status, and if Jesus tarries, he may just become the new devil. It's not only you who fears your father, even the devil does. Thank God that fatherhood doesn't end there. Halleluiah.

Earthly disappointments or standards must not be used to judge your intimacy with the real Father. Nothing must stop you from embracing your Father. (My earthly father's sins will not stop me from getting my freedom. I forgive him, I let him go. No grudges, for that is the path of Satan. That is the devil's kingdom mentality. I pray for my earthly father even when I know the basest of things he has done. And I love him unconditionally. His sins are his. I will not share in his sins. I refuse. **I refuse to compose a song about what my father did and sing it for the rest of eternity. No, no, no.**

But pastor my father did this. My father did that.

So? You want me to give him a medal or what? You want my sympathy? I don't have any to waste! Corporal get up and march forward! There is no devil that will hold me back from loving my Dad. Love him. This may even extend to spiritual fathers. If my pastor hurt me I refuse to dwell on it. They may have hurt you very much, but refuse to nurse it. Some spiritual parents are destructive. How we need more sensible spiritual parents in our times.

Forgive whoever has wronged you. Pray for them. *But pastor that's with all respect a stupid idea. I've been hurt.* I totally agree with you. It sounds stupid. That is what we are, to the world, stupid. However, there is great wisdom. I know you do not feel like doing it. **But who says you should feel?** We do not move by senses but by faith. Take time to pray. Let us agree together. Together we make an undefeatable team.

PRAYER

*Father, in the name of Jesus
I ask you to strengthen me in the
inner man by the Holy Spirit. I
forgive my Father for what he did
to me. It is not how I feel but the
faith I apply right now in forgiving him.
I shall never allow the devil to take
me back on that route again. Father I
let go of any grudge, pain or bitterness
I have held against him. I set him free.
Heavenly Father I ask you to forgive
my father and open his eyes that he
may know you. Let him know Jesus,
the only True Savior. I thank you for
giving me the Holy Spirit who is
my Guide, Strengthener and Comforter.
Thank you Dad.
Amen.*

Wonderful. You've done it. Nothing is impossible. Now we continue...

God's power is at your fingertips and it is far much greater than you'll ever figure out. In fact the sooner you start doing all you can to grasp this the better. The Word of God is final. It is more than dynamite. **Stop struggling with unbelief.** The Bible says God has blessed you with all spiritual blessings in the heavenly places.

Heavenly places is not a place in the next life. **It means dominion in the now! Where God's Word has put you that**

is your real place. Your true position. **Do you know that the world is run on words?** In fact, the Universe itself came into existence by the Word. That is how powerful and important God's Word is. God's Kingdom functions on the Word. The earth functions on words. The devil's kingdom functions on words. It all depends on whose word you follow. I would rather follow God's Word who created the universe to change whatever thing I am facing. **In fact, the word 'universe' means one verse.** God created the universe using one verse; *Let there be!* **But how many verses directly relate to your situation in the Bible?** If the universe can be fashioned in one verse and God gives you thousands of verses concerning your situation, surely it must budge! I know it budges!!

I.   BABES IN THE WORD

I forgot about the miracle of unbelief. Many are in bondage because of unbelief. Unbelief is a miracle because it manages to do something beyond comprehension.

> Psalm 78:41 *Yea, they turned back and tempted God, and __limited__ the Holy One of Israel.* (Emphasis added)

It takes a miracle to limit a Limitless God. Do you know who was being limited there? God, the Holy Spirit. Unbelief limits The Limitless. In Mathematics we could say, **'It makes the Infinite a subset of the Finite'.** Now if that is not a miracle there will never ever be one! The Lord Jesus before going said when the Holy Spirit comes He will convict the world of what? Sin. What sin? The sin of not believing in Him. Unbelief. The ultimate sin. There is something about unbelief and the world system. A calculated design for the rise of the Antichrist. We are seeing a great rise in deception. People coming up with ways to draw many from Jesus the Christ. For example, there is an interest to try and figure out the actual appearance of Jesus. I am sure they will come up with a face. And the world will be told this is the actual appearance of Jesus. But suppose that face is the face of the long awaited Antichrist, the devil's favorite child? Wouldn't that lead the whole world to the devil's feet, since we are expecting his *eminence's* imminent ascendancy to power? We must be extra careful. Extra careful. True Christians must not fall for the hoax of the shroud of Turin. We have been told it is the burial cloth of the Lord Jesus. And Jesus' face is imprinted on it. Ultimate proof has proven this not to be true. Though now the shroud story is pure comedy. We are told, by some genius, the cloth the scientists tested was not a piece or part of the shroud, but just some other cloth. Ha ha ha. I am sure they tested a chitenge from Mulungushi Textiles. Circus. On a serious note, whose cloth is this? Could it be the cloth of a magician of old? A man who is one of the pioneers of Freemasonry? Grand Master Knight Templar Jacques de Molay? He had been to the Holy land, remember? Yes, yes, Michael, I have heard of the Edessa story. How some disciple of Jesus fled with a cloth to Turkey. And from the **factory of burial cloths** of Jesus they had, this one is the authentic burial cloth. Hooray! But even if this story was stretched way back, 2000 years ago, it does not still bring Jesus in the picture!

It is great, to see everyone, finally turning religious. Is it the reason we see graven images and symbols everywhere? Even the cross is now a problem. There are so many satanic ritual crosses and you see many 'Christians' with them. What kind of rubbish is that? I have been seeing so many ministers of the 'gospel' with devilish crosses. Ignorance? No, calculated deception. *Vampires.* Our heroes and heroines today, including the clergy are telling us that Jesus is not the only way to the Father. *We know on whose side they are.* **It is either Jesus is a liar or our heroes and heroines are hardcore liars!** What do you call that? Thank you my Dear Anne. **The law of excluded middle!** There is no neutral ground. Jesus cannot be correct and our cult personalities also correct. Nay. What does that wonderful Bible prophecy say?

Jeremiah 32:39 *And I will give them one heart, and one way,*

that they may fear me for ever, for the good of them,
and of their children after them

How many ways did the Almighty God we claim to teach others about promise us? And hasn't He fulfilled that? Do not compound your misery. Quit your pastoral positions. At least your judgement will be lighter. Friend do not flow with the wicked tide. Haven't you seen the claim that the *Lord Jesus is coming soon* intensifying? Why all the fuss? The same people who deny He is not the only way are telling us to get ready for his soon coming? Sounds fishy. There is another savior. If Jesus could tell Christians not to be crazy about dates, how could the world tell us the Lord is coming soon, and others even set dates? Unless... it is the impostor! Many people of the cloth are telling us about the imminent coming of the Lord Jesus. That looks so sweet to the average Christian. But when put under serious scrutiny, the Jesus they talk about is the Antichrist. Since they have been talking about it, the world will be ready to embrace him when he appears. To their peril. But for us, we will depend on the awesome Word of the King of kings, The ONLY TRUE AND HOLY WAY. **His Word is the final authority.**

Just look at the billions of dollars being spent on trying to get a few words from soothsayers, clairvoyants. Carrot (or is it tarot?) card readers, palm readers...many believe so much in the words of these people not the Word of God. Words are important. However, there is one word above all. The Word of God. Never live without it. Dear you do not need to run across the globe to find out about your future. God the one who created you has not left you blank concerning His will for you. Ephesians 1:9, 5:17 emphasize that God's will for you is clear. If you do not know His Will He is unhappy! An heir (you) should see his Father's Will for himself! How do you do that? By searching the scriptures. The devil will do everything possible to keep you away from knowing the contents of God's Will. But your Lawyer Jesus wants you to know. Do not give the swindler a foothold. Eph. 4:27. Ignorance gives Satan a foothold. Ignorance grieves the Holy Spirit.

Knowledge of the Divine Will is your greatest treasure or asset in this life. As a new creation, there is more to you than you can ever imagine or grasp. No wonder God has to give you the mind of Christ to understand it.

> 1 Corinthians 2:16b *...But we have the mind of Christ.*

Look at what the Bible says about you. Take a serious study. **You are supernatural.** You are born-again. Born from above. That is why Satan is so jealous of you that every bit of him vibrates with undiluted abhorrence. He suffers from ulcers. All he had, has gone. And he thought he had been to a place where no one else could ascend. The only thing he thought possible was being replaced when he fell. But he challenged **The Infinite**. There are more levels beyond Satan's understanding. That is where God has put you. Satan cannot believe what his evil eye balls are telling him. Your presence alone is torture, and I mean that in a literal sense. What more when you exercise your God given rights? Ephesians 2:10 says you were created for good works. When you hear 'good works' what comes to your mind? Feeding the hungry, clothing the naked? That's good, however there is more to it than meets the eye. There are the spiritually hungry and spiritually naked. **In Acts 10:38 Jesus moved in the good works. That is what Dad wants you to flow in. Nothing less**. God's investment in you is beyond zillions of dollars. No exaggeration. Do you know what is in you? No. You don't. If only you knew even a bit. But God doesn't want you to know a bit. He wants you to know it all. Your link is the Holy Spirit.

Many read Ephesians 1:19 without pausing to really get what the Word is saying. The Bible says the power at work in you is not less than the power that God used in raising Jesus from the dead. Hmm. And God didn't just raise Jesus He crowned Him too. He made Jesus sit above all Power and Dominion. When He was crowned you were crowned. And the devil seeing that he hates you. You are seated in Christ Jesus. In English ...(your name) you are in power. There is no high-ranking demon to fear. Allow me to put it crudely, the highest-ranking 'demon', Satan, is far much below you. If you are above the master, the pawns are no match. Do you know why Satan preys on infants? They cannot talk even when the **Word** is near!

Deuteronomy 30:14a *But the word is very nigh*
unto thee, in thy mouth, and
in thy heart...

Witchcraft the in-thing now, is wreaking havoc among believers. Frustration everywhere. I experienced it. Everything I did went down the drain. My best always produced the worst. I had a mixture of Godly prayers and demonic prayers. I quoted the Bible and after a few minutes, I would start quoting the devil. Murmuring. Ever been there?

Murmuring is quoting the devil don't you ever do it. Murmuring is demonic prayer. It is the devil's praise. **I locked on and have never looked back since.** *From that moment I have been hearing murmuring from the other camp. That's the way it should be.* But babes, what do they do when things aren't going their way? Good guess. They cry. In fact they go beyond crying. They have one principle. If I've no peace nobody is gonna get it ! And they put their little feet down. Attend to them or else you ain't sleeping. Infants are destructive. **They want their way even when they don't know any way.** Are you ready to grow up? The Lord Jesus asked me a simple question, which needs careful consideration. I'm passing it on to you. **'Did the Holy Spirit lose any of His power when He came to live in you?'** Friend that question applies to you. Why are you powerless? Why is the enemy chasing you around? Why is it that when you speak God's Word there is no power? Think about it. 1 John 4:4 Greater is He...God is great in me. I'm born again. **Friend the doctrine you receive will either help you or crush you.** Paul emphasized that to Timothy.

1 Timothy 4:16 *Watch your life and doctrine closely.*
Persevere in them, because if you do, you will
save both yourself and your

hearers. (NIV)

Note that it is not enough to watch your life and doctrine. Watch your life and your **doctrine closely!!** What a word. Shallowness is not holiness. I have been saying that for the past thirteen years. As you study the Holy Spirit will reveal something which will take you out of the doldrums. Revelations from the Word are not evil. Extremism is not spirituality either. Before men of God criticize others, they should first grasp what has been put forth. For some of them do not know that what they criticize, out of ignorance, is their key to success. The Holy Spirit is your link to the wonderland. And that wonderland is right where you are, but you need your eyes to be opened. God is not just ready to give you grace. He is more than ready to give you more grace! James 4:6. In fact, the Bible mentions Grace multiplied in another verse in the Book of Peter. There is nothing impossible with you.

> Numbers 23:23 *Surely there is no enchantment against Jacob,*
> *neither is there any divination against Israel:*
> *according to this time it shall be said of*
> *Jacob and of Israel, What*
> *hath God wrought!*

There is no 'enchantment'. The word actually means serpent! There is no serpent against you. **And the devil is a serpent!** Sorcery cannot work. It must not work.

II. BABES IN SOCIAL LIFE

✓ Spiritual Snakes

Psalm 74:14, Acts 16:16

> Acts 16:16 *Once when we were going to the place of prayer, we*
> *were met by a slave girl who had a spirit by which she*
> *predicted the future. She earned a great deal*

of money for her owners by
fortune-telling. (NIV)

(From the scripture we see that demons can, to some degree tell the future. That speaks volumes with our insatiable demand for 'pastor prophesy, pastor prophesy). The spirit that was in the girl was the **Python spirit.** This is a familiar spirit. It gets close to the leadership. It desires to associate with men and women of God. But it is a dangerous **controlling** spirit. The language seems right, but discern the motive.

✓ Seducing Spirits

Genesis 3, 2 Corinthians. 10:4–5.

2 Corinthians 10:5a *Casting down imaginations, and every high thing*
that exalteth itself against the knowledge of God,
and bringing into captivity every
thought to the obedience
of Christ…

2 Corinthians 10:4 *(For the arms with which we are fighting are not those of the flesh,*
but are strong before God for the destruction of high places); 5
Putting an end to reasonings, and every high
thing which is lifted up against the knowledge of
God, and causing every thought to come
under the authority of Christ;

(BBE)

High places are destroyed as we demolish reasoning! **High places are satanic altars.** Thank God we have the ability to destroy them! The world has come under the sway of this demon. This spirit of reasoning or imaginations is very strong. It reasons you out of the safety zone. It trivializes God's Word and work. Then it offers alternatives. Many are turning to the worship of their long forgotten ancestors and spirits. Cultures are being encouraged. We are rediscovering our heritage. Hooray! Yes certain things about our cultures are good. But there are others that are clearly not right. Even if one is not a Christian, one can tell bad culture from good culture. *Well, sometimes.* In the name of our much treasured culture, one genius thought of coming up with a rape day!

Keyworth, are you on meth?

Dear, I don't even know how to spell crystal meth.

Yes there is an official rape day on this sweet planet. Some authorities felt, this would benefit society. Reality is sometimes stranger than fiction. What happens on that day? Well, people rape! Rape as in forced sex. *This is a great law.* I see women NGOs taking guns marching. *This is terrible. Men want to use us. How dare they do this to us. Keyworth, where the hell is this imaginary place you are talking about? We want to go and free the women. It's disgusting.* I have got news for you my darling women. It's the women who rape! Women are the ones raping men. Men don't. The women will ambush men and take turns raping the men. Two on one, three on one and *even hundred on one if he is very handsome, like you sir!* The main idea is to reduce infidelity. That way the women will be faithful for the rest of the year! Amen. This is one brilliant law. Ingenious culture. Aren't we just smart? This has taken care of adultery and diseases. I won't be tempted to talk about illegitimate pregnancies. On this day men hide from women. Girl power. *I pray, by the great mercies of God, I don't receive calls from lonely men asking for details.*

Not to be out done, another smart guy came up with the winning cultural formula. This is astounding. Before you even read it, stand up and clap for this genius. I don't even know how to pen this. On your wedding night, after all the fasting and praying to avoid fornication, you are told to hold your fire. Just for one more day. Well, for the bridegroom-turned-hubby. Why? **The experienced father of the man, has to take the young lady for some high performance lessons.** Yes. The father of the man sleeps with the girl to test her goodness in bed. He is testing (and tasting) for his son! *Smart Dad, how we just need more of them.*

Keyworth, are you sure you are a real pastor? Why are you lying? This can't happen. What kind of a custom is that?

Dear, I can't comment on this custom. If I do, God will wonder if I am still a Christian. Look at my lips, zipped.

Any zealous men ready to go through this process? Brave ladies, yes, with the father of your man? I see hands everywhere. We are civilized indeed. **But what is more shocking is that this practice is not confined to one country!!!** Then we have Christians pursuing **naked** beaches. Christians want to experience the life of Adam and Eve. They don't want any strand of cotton on their holy bodies. Clothes, they argue, came after sin. So nudity is actually purity! There is a Christian group or section of the 'church' that practices nudity. **In fact there are various groups of Christians who do this.** They worship naked. I met a gentleman who belonged to such. And he told me, they are the true worshippers of God. And he really wanted me to join them. Whoa! A place full of naked people worshipping? My hyper active mind can't process that! It keeps on jamming. These Christians don't wear clothes! Reasoning is the devil's stronghold. Be careful what you hear. Most of the Christian teachings today have been mixed with New Age reasonings. It's time to grow up! The New Agers have in some places counterfeited the Church teachings that it takes close scrutiny to see the difference. And by New Age I encompass all that has to do with the New World Order. For the true meaning of New Age is the same as New World Order. New Age is a reference to the New Age of God The Son, who is Horus, the one-eyed (third eye) world savior!

Nobody can claim to be ignorant of the great happenings in our days. Reasoning people into destruction is the in-thing now. Let's take a microscope and have a serious look at this spirit of reasoning. There have been myths and shrouded in the myths are real issues which the ordinary man seems not to get. There is an unholy trinity, which some suppose is holy. This unholy trinity is represented by a triangle and an eye inside the triangle.

The triangle represents Osiris—the Father, Isis—the sister and wife and Horus—the son. **Though embedded in 'myth' this trinity is very real.** Osiris is Satan himself, Isis is the *female* demon (God Mother) and Horus the Antichrist, through whom Satan manifests or reigns on earth.

Our greatest focus is on Isis, the *female* demon. This demon is Satan's deputy or vice president. This demon is peculiar in that it oversees certain secret societies. Its demands are beyond the ordinary person's understanding. The training one has to undergo, our commandos cannot fathom. The wildest imagination of evil or ordeal you can come up with does not compare to its simplest demand or task. Anyone who divulges the secrets entrusted to them are tormented beyond their human ability to handle pain. Emotionally and physically you are broken to smithereens. It's hard, very hard to leave her grip. The fear she pumps in you, is abnormal. And what many do not know, this demon, is in charge of three aspects of life. Please, am begging you, don't forget what you are about to read.

One of the greatest secrets of Satan is that this demon Isis, is the one directly in charge of Religion, Science and Philosophy! It promises to reveal deep insight or the highest level of enlightenment in Religion, Science and Philosophy. The members of secret societies MUST be Religious scientific philosophers to be deemed enlightened!

The Antichrist has mastered all these three more than any man alive! This is the highest deception point! The antichrist is actually the most deceived Satan worshipper. Religion, goes beyond the borders of a nation. People are more loyal to their religion than to their country. And that applies to science and philosophy. Carry out your own research; look at the real things that control lives, things that individuals are more loyal to. You won't miss these three. Today there is a pull towards uniting these three. This has been one much guarded secret, but the times are ripe to start the open take over. The common man has to be introduced to this or else! For a properly enlightened soul must be all three. I can assure you, there are very very few people who are not religious on earth. Secret societies are serious religions. Ladies and gentlemen, not every religious thing is holy and not every scientific discovery is for your benefit. Isis is the one dispensing some of this evil technology.

> One of the greatest secrets of Satan is that this demon Isis, is the one directly in charge of Religion, Science and Philosophy!

Give the devil's deputy a good offer, she will give you a 'discovery' and the world will think you are a genius, when you are not! Some positions in society and discoveries we pant for, are very **costly.** One courageous simple satanist walked up to me and said, 'Pastor, accept the fact that Satanism is just a science.' I wasn't surprised because that's what they actually call it! Divine science! They mix normal science and witchcraft. *And philosophy?* Philosophy, hmm.

Our pulpits are full of mercenaries, from the kingdom of darkness. These philosophers have introduced another gospel. It is common sense. If there is another Christ on the horizon, there must be another gospel. Christians are confused, they don't know who is who and they do not seem to know where the New Age doctrines come in. Many believe philosophy instead of the Word of the great I AM, JEHOVAH. For philosophy has replaced God's Word. Make the people feel comfortable in sin, give them a social gospel, while the noose tightens around their necks. What are we learning in schools, is it not many empty philosophies that despise the true Creator and His Son, Jesus Christ? Isis chose the core areas of human life, religion, science and philosophy. These are things that affect us every day! Isis, that mother god, whom many have embraced under various names and titles, is pulling multitudes in her dragnet. Charles Darwin, remember the fella? He stepped on the podium to solve the problem for all the rebels with a philosophy, now coated as science. The Theory Of Evolution. In a trice Charles Darwin became a hero. All those who hated Christianity, but had nothing to throw at it jumped and joined the bandwagon. What followed is almost a coup de tat in Christianity. Empty shells of poor imitations of theologians started teaching evolution as gospel truth.

Others started throwing away certain portions of the Bible for evolution. **According to this assumption of Evolution, chance will lead to a net increase in the order and complexity seen in the world and Universe.** But modern science and advancement in various fields have proved evolution, the worst hoax since creation. **The result of what they suggest is ALWAYS DECREASE and DESTRUCTION of order.** Among the informed Evolution is not even whispered. The greatest scientist of all times is Jehovah, no one will come close to matching Him! Satan and Isis are just fooling themselves. That, they know better. Evolution has consistently failed. The Holy Spirit comes down and reasons with us, at a kindergarten level in the Word of God when He declares

Hebrews 3:4 *For every house has a builder;*
but the builder of all
things is God.
(BBE)

If you can't understand this scripture, your IQ is abnormally high! Ever seen a hurricane before? How many houses were created by hurricanes? Ever seen an earthquake? How many skyscrapers with furniture came out of it? Order out of chaos? **Ever seen a house which was never built by a human being, but by chance?** Chance drew the architectural plan and put in all the details. The ventilation and air cons, because chance had the weather in mind. *Chance must be a smart fella.* Who knows of such a house? What about the universe, which is even more complex? **Bang!** By chance! Pure accidents. Everything was set in order just like that. Clap for yourself. You must be very smart to believe that. Atheists say they don't believe in God. I say I don't believe in atheists! I am sorry, I am yet to hear and meet someone who is really an atheist! I know, not in this life, maybe in the next! How can I believe a fella who does not speak **logically,** but by chance? Atheists who happen to be products of chance cannot speak logic. Anything they say is by chance or accident not reason or intelligence! If you are discussing football don't be surprised he starts talking about rockets! In their world, there is no reasoning. That's why I get confused when they try to reason! I am sure they reason by accident! They talk by accident. **Friend, I don't just believe in these Darwin atheists.**

Romans 1:20 *For the invisible things of him from the creation of the world are clearly seen, being understood by the things that are made, even his eternal power and Godhead; so that they are without excuse :21 Because that, when they knew God, they glorified him not as God, neither were thankful; but became vain in their imaginations, and their foolish heart was darkened.*

No one has an excuse! Everyone knows something about God. **EVERYONE!** They have just given themselves to vain imagination which the devil capitalizes on and hardens their hearts. And you think they don't know God.

John 1:9 *That was the true Light, which lighteth every man that cometh into the world.*

Here we see the Bible clearly telling us that every human being has some degree of light about God. Bible scholars have debated whether this scripture means the true Light is the one coming into the world or it is every person who comes into the world who is lit by this true Light. Aisha, I believe both sides are correct.

This scripture is similar to Isaiah 59:19. We have wasted time debating whether it is this or that interpretation. But both are correct. We just need to understand what the Lord is saying to us.

Isaiah 59:19 *So shall they fear the name of the LORD from the west, and his glory from the rising of the sun. When the enemy shall come in like a flood, the Spirit of the LORD shall lift up a standard against him.* (NKJV)

Some say it is the enemy who comes like a flood, others say it is the Spirit of the Lord who comes like a flood. It doesn't make any difference. I love both. For the following reasons.

✓ **If the former has to be taken, we see how the devil is raging with madness to destroy God's own. But the Spirit of God, who is Creator and God Almighty effortlessly lifts up a standard or puts the devil to flight! Jesus spoke of the EASE with which devil's are cast out in Luke 11:20!**

✓ **If it is the Spirit of God who comes like a flood, it reveals how jealous God is. He doesn't want anything to touch you, because you are precious!**

David described it this way:

Psalm 18:6 *In my distress I called upon the LORD, And cried out to my God; He heard my voice from His temple, And my cry came before Him, even to His ears.* ⁷ *Then the earth shook and trembled; The foundations of the hills also quaked and were shaken, Because He was angry.* (NKJV)

Don't play with God when it comes to His children. You will forever regret it! God goes crazy over His own. It's like playing with an elephant's young one. You don't want to do that. Don't make it angry. When it comes charging, it will show you the real meaning of treading! Trees literally jump out of the way! Whichever way you look at this scripture, one thing is clear, our God shows up, and puts the devil to flight! *Now you know the devil is a coward! He sprints!!* It doesn't matter what Satan tries to confuse people with, we know him. And his little strongholds are no match for the Spirit of God! We are not ignorant. The devil is not as big as he claims to be!

III. BABES IN SPIRITUAL WARFARE

Over the years, we have left the coats of infancy and are matching on into maturity. But there was a time when we would talk about the strongholds of the devil. Our eyes would pop out of their sockets because we felt so unworthy even to talk about them. Only serious, mighty men of God could talk about them, so we thought. That was giving respect to a whitewashed enemy. Don't you ever glorify the devil. There is no stronghold in the Universe like the one I'm about to show you. **Never!!!!**

> Psalm 9:9 *The LORD is a refuge for the oppressed, a <u>stronghold</u> in times of trouble.* (Emphasis added)

A stronghold is a fortress. A castle. A barrack. An arsenal. A modern military base. God is our fortress! Halleluiah. But that is not what I intend giving you an idea about.

> Colossians 1:19 *For it pleased the Father that in him should all fullness dwell...*

Did you see that? God compacted the **sum total** of His Greatness and **total being** in Jesus. **Jesus is God's Stronghold.** Is there anything stronger than God's Stronghold? Demons never smiled when Jesus confronted them. They said bye bye to their kids and wives and wrote their wills. They knew they were not coming back. They made funeral arrangements, got insurance cover and chose songs to be played on the funeral, why? They were going to meet God's Stronghold. The devil solemnly patted them on the back, the hour of reckoning had come. All the fullness of God dwells in Him! Child of God shout halleluiah. *But is that the end?* We are just warming up. Do you know that demons literally begged Jesus? That is what a mature child of God does, demonstrates his calling. The good news is 1 John 4:17. As Jesus is, so am I (mention your name point at yourself). The opposite is true for those who worship Satan. As the Antichrist is, so are they. Nothing should surprise you from now on. I'm not ashamed to shout halleluiah to my KING, JESUS! The devil can go and hang himself with his wife I do not care! *Now don't say I've taught you that demons choose songs to be played on their funerals and they get insurance cover. You are not a baby, are you?*

Okay. It was the Father's Pleasure for Jesus to have the fullness of God in Him. Look at these two scriptures and be your own judge.

Colossians 1:19 *For it pleased the Father that in him should <u>all fulness dwell</u>;*
(emphasis added)

Ephesians 3:19 *...that ye might <u>be filled</u> with <u>all the fulness of God</u>.*
(emphasis added)

Did your eyes catch that? You missed it. Okay here it comes in slow mo.

Colossians 2:9 *For in Christ all the fullness of the Deity lives in bodily form*

10 and you have been given fullness in Christ... (NIV)

Verse 9 is important, but the most important **right now** is verse 10! Everyone has no problem with verse 9, even the devil has accepted it, but verse 10 he doesn't want you to grasp it. He doesn't. But this is what you must get with all your total being. Settle for nothing less. **That fullness that the Father has given to Christ, has also been given to you.**

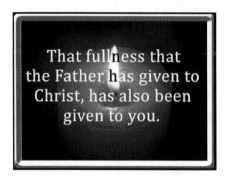

This is what Satan does not want you to know. **The picture you have about yourself and about God are poles apart.** God really loves you practically. What do you think is The Father's pleasure for you? The former is about Jesus the latter about you. Let us put it this way.

✓ In you dwells the Holy Spirit 1 Cor. 6:19

✓ In you dwells the Lord Jesus Eph. 3:17

✓ In you dwells the Father Ephesians 4:6

So, is Ephesians 3:19 and Colossians 2:10 too hot to handle? **You are the Strongest Stronghold in existence right now in the universe!** I know you missed it deliberately. Listen you are God's Ultimate Arsenal. Don't look around you. It's you........... (your name). **The devil will give anything for you not to know that he has been stripped of everything and you are the greatest force in the universe!!!!! God has compacted the sum total of His Greatness and total being in you!** Do you understand what you are reading? **The Bible is out of this world!** No wonder the Pharisees would get shocked and offended by Jesus' teachings. They sounded nothing less than preposterous. There is another scripture that makes the Bible either abnormally sweet or completely false. Look at this

Ephesians 3:20 *Now unto him that is able to do exceeding*

abundantly above all that we ask or think,
according to the power that
worketh in us

Paul *ran out* of words when the Holy Spirit told him to pen this scripture. He was in shock. He uses the words

- ✓ **Exceeding**

- ✓ **Abundantly**

- ✓ **Above all that we ask**.

Notice that if God is able to do exceeding my request that is mind blowing, but he combines **exceeding, abundantly** and **above all that we ask,** and to blow our minds to smithereens he states **or think!** What is beyond what I think that God is ready to do? **Are we really living life to the full, or are we just wallowing in shallowness for lack of knowledge?** What kind of things are we going to experience once we break our limits? We limit what to expect from God. Friend God is bigger than we can comprehend. This is the proof. Every time some people look at such appalling scriptures they want to water it down so that it suits their limited thinking, let the scripture speak for itself! Now get this icing on the cake. **That power to accomplish what we ask or think is not coming from heaven.** Stop looking up. That power is in you! I am not talking about the foolish New Age—Christ in you, meaning higher self. No. That is nonsense. Oh God. If this is true, which it is because you are the greatest arsenal in the universe, then let's stop living below par. **The sky can never be the limit.** Is this heating up your heart? *I can't blame you for pinching yourself, I went through the same process.* How could you have lived like a refugee when you have all this at your disposal? The devil doesn't want you to know this, but now you know. This is the basis for saying, "Greater is He that is in me than the one in the world." I am God's Fortress. And this is what the devil sees all the time. Wonderful.

Perhaps this might bring some fear and trepidation. With revelation comes responsibility. Learn this: Somebody once said if you pray very much and read the Word demons will increase their attack. So it is better to be moderate. I said no. That is not biblical. The Bible says resist the devil and he will flee! It doesn't say he will come with his uncles and cousins. Of course, I understood what the dear saint was trying to say. The devil plays psychology whenever you start serious praying. Take it as a sign of his defeat. He is panicking. When you see abnormal challenges in your life and you are living rightly, then your double doors have been opened for you. The devil is putting in his last because the inevitable has come. Whatever the devil has tried to postpone will definitely come to pass now. You may look stupid and people laugh at you but know this; you will laugh and laugh heartily and those who laughed at you? They will be praising you. God has promised that you will never be put to shame. Now what does that mean in English? The shame you have passed through is nothing compared to your uplifting. Just dig in your heels. Persistence remember? **The only devil you must know is a fleeing devil. That is the devil's official position.** I'm not kidding. **James 4:7.** So who's in charge? You are. You have been given the mandate to rule as you obediently serve Jesus. The devil is not in charge.

Perspective, Persistence and constant Confession keep you victorious. You do not count your victory by the physical circumstances. Do not be short-sighted, remember Elisha's servant? You are victorious all the time. Just be immovable! 1 Corinthians 15:57. I remember we were having a discussion and a friend said, *'It appears the devil is ruling'*. I responded, *'It all depends on the kingdom one is in. In my kingdom Jesus rules'*. The devil is not ruling in your life child of God. The devil cannot even accidentally take me into his kingdom. I'll pass through his throne and leave behind a fire which not even his fire fighters can put out. I am not simple! I know who I am and whose I am. The devil took Jesus into his kingdom, he has never forgotten the consequences. He cannot, even allow such a thought to cross his mind, why? **Can he dare take the Jesus in me again into his kingdom? That would**

shorten his already shortened life span. The only devil I know is a fleeing devil. Search the scriptures.

> Isaiah 27:1a *In that day the Lord with his hard and great and strong sword will punish Leviathan the fleeing serpent...* (ESV)

That is the devil you must know. A ruling one? No. A running one. And for your information, leviathan is still a very active name in Satanism. It is not for a mythological monster. I am not trying to be disrespectful to anyone, but why the hell do we gobble information from questionable experts? Why are most children of darkness defining what we should believe in?

Pastor Keyworth, Professor Kamikaze has discovered that Jesus was distributing condoms.

Really?

Whoa, we respect him, it must be true. And not only that, Professor Kamikaze has discovered leviathan does not exist.

You and Professor Kamikaze are very intelligent.

No matter what people say about Jesus, He is Lord of lords and King of kings. And who says leviathan lives in a laboratory? When Jesus looked at his troops, He was appalled at their dullness. He couldn't wait for the Holy Spirit to come and do something.

> Luke 16:8 *...for the children of this world are in their generation wiser than the children of light.*

Now the Holy Spirit has come and we seem to have become even more intelligent than before. **What is wrong with us?!!! I fully agree with the Lord Jesus, we seem to be no match for** the devil's brood. **While they are focused and well taught, we refuse to learn and unfortunately have now become a very poor imitation of a faded photocopy. In China some people pirate anything. Except us. It shows how low we have sank! I am very shocked to realize we don't even qualify to be pirated!** Leviathan is real. And billions have gone after him. What is the kundalini serpent in yoga, if not leviathan? Don't play with fire! Spiritual matters, the Bible declares are spiritually discerned! The natural man, from the kingdom of man cannot understand them. And the spiritual man from the devil's kingdom, he will confuse you. Those in the kingdom of darkness are smart. How many have fallen for yoga? They are told to reach higher self consciousness or something like that. The point? To reach a level of being a god. Why? Thank you David. So that when **aliens** from other planets or galaxies come, they do not take advantage of you, for you have power. Aliens? We save that for another day, but it becomes interesting.

Power to attain god status is what you pursue in yoga. Power that you have been kept away from by an evil Christian God. The Father, The Holy Spirit and Jesus are gods who do not desire us to attain this god status, but Satan does. Yoga is encouraged in the kingdom of darkness. I know this very well. If yoga carries light, the kingdom of darkness cannot encourage it, the way it does. There is a fissure the devil has entered through. It's beginning to sound like the Adam and Eve story to me. And the devil, though he is the father of lies, he seems to recycle his lies! Satan loves us and he is trying to protect us from the aliens who are coming. In fact Satan is the true god, not God the Father, The Son and The Holy Spirit. **It is clear from this that the more you practice yoga you follow what Satan wants and pit yourself against the True God.**

It is that simple! Common sense.

What I am putting before you are spiritual matters. We don't need a UN resolution. We must discern. Wisen up, dearest. To all who love the Lord Jesus and all He stands for, maintain Isaiah 27:1a. The devil is that fleeing serpent. So if the devil runs from the Word of God, then take advantage. Declare it. The word 'fleeing' is the same word 'fugitive'. The devil is a fugitive! Halleluiah!!! (*Now that you know what are you going to do?*) The Word is special. Speak it. Speaking has a special effect on you and the surrounding. Speaking the Word affects the three kingdoms. God is happy, the devil is sad and you have your answer. What else would a person want? A happy Jesus and a sad devil. Sounds fair to me. The Word is only active when spoken. **The Word of God is voice activated.** When the Bible mentions the sword of the Spirit in Ephesians 6, it is not talking about the Bible. **The Bible is not the sword of the Spirit. The sword of the Spirit is a verse or scripture that you take and use at a particular moment. The sword of the Spirit is a word in motion, the word that is coming from your mouth.** Putting your Bible under your pillow before going to bed will not stop nightmares. In fact, the devil will be so happy that he will give you a bonus package—'*daymares*'.

Quote the scriptures. As you quote, you activate them. All the promises of God are 'yes' and the amen is spoken by who? You! Activate your spiritual account today.

Remember God used one verse on the Universe, but on you, He has used Multiverses. The promises are inexhaustible. Now is your moment to bask in the multi-faceted Wisdom of God your Dad... you are God's favorite. You have received favor. Live it. Now that you know you are a power house let me give you a tip on the power at work in your life. Just a tip. In your life and in your family, there is ...

8.

THE GENERATIONAL ANOINTING

Isaiah 59:21 *As for me, this is my covenant with them, saith the LORD; My spirit that is upon thee, and my words which I have put in thy mouth, shall not depart out of thy mouth, nor out of the mouth of thy seed, nor out of the mouth of thy seed's seed, saith the LORD, from henceforth and forever. 60:1 Arise, shine; for thy light is come, and the glory of the LORD is risen upon thee.*

A debate has been raging on for some time now. **Are there generational curses, if so what does one do?** Others will say there are no such things. But we know for a long time children of God have tottered under *generational curses.* **Is it possible for a curse to work in the life of a child of God?** Answers to both of these questions must fully be understood to avoid confusion. **To start with, it is important to realize that a curse could be running in your family because someone else made a covenant with the enemy on your behalf.** For example if your father or grandfather makes a covenant with the kingdom of darkness then all the offspring are under that covenant. Two parties, your father or grandfather and the devil enforce that covenant. The physical and the spiritual parties, two kingdoms at work. In short, that family has come under the covering of that demon. All the affairs of the family are in its hands. The family may get material things even fame or power but it does not forget to pay its dues, for example, at a certain time someone in the family has to miscarry or die. The secret may not be known to everyone in that family and it is usually passed on when the person who made the covenant is about to die. Remember the three kingdoms? Nothing legitimizes a covenant like blood. **Do**

you still remember that all the covenants we looked at in the three kingdoms involve blood?

Automatically, the person who covenanted with the devil is the spiritual leader of the family. But what happens when this person's offspring becomes born again? *You beloved, you become born again.* You do three things.

- ✓ **You defy and break the covenant with the devil.**

- ✓ **You establish yourself as the new spiritual leader of the family.**

- ✓ **You introduce another spiritual covering to your family, Jesus the Christ.**

Your father for example, if he is the one who made the covenant loses the spiritual position to you. Are you getting this? As long as you are there that person cannot lead, **because the covenant of death is less than the covenant of life.** And the kingdom of God is superior to all the other kingdoms.

> Psalm 103:19 *The LORD has prepared his throne in the heavens; and his kingdom rules over all.*

The kingdom you belong to rules over all!!! Halleluiah. **I repeat, the devil is not in charge!** The other covenant is dead. Listen, you are a king and a priest, see Revelation 1:5-6. If you look at that scripture further you will see that all dominion or rule on earth **is** subject to Jesus. The devil is not in charge. Don't fear him. As a king, the first territory of leadership is your family. And that's when things become sweet. Prepare for high-powered tension. The enemy will not take it lying down.

> Ecclesiastes 10:16a *Woe to thee, O land, when thy king is a child...*

Look at this. 'Woe' is a curse. Upon what? The land. The curse will seem to linger even when there has been a change of leadership upon your territory, why? Because the new king is not a trained soldier. He eats when he is supposed to fast. He mixes with the wrong people. He does not pray instead he wants a 'quickie' like the old favorite, the mealtime prayer, 5 seconds and it is finished. When you become born-again you automatically have an abnormal struggle spiritually. Your subjects are not happy. Many give up out of ignorance. They leave their territory. **The king is a child.** Don't be immature. Take your stance. Pray like never before.

But pastor, we live by grace, so we just pray for three minutes and read the Bible for two minutes. We are busy people.

Ha ha ha. Whoever told you that is the devil's first cousin! If Jesus could pray the way He did, Mark 6:46-48, we can't ignore prayer. That is why we have become weak and are unable to know the lies of the enemy. The devil fears prayer. **He fears a praying Christian!** Stop being immature. We are not novices. **We know how demons become weak in the presence of a praying Christian.** The more you pray the weaker they become! Brethren get this secret and let it be etched in your soul. Don't flee. Stand your ground. The struggle does not end when you flee. The enemy will pursue you until you are his subject. Stop being immature and fight for your life! Immature or not the struggle is on don't you know that? Are you a king in exile? Shame. It is also very interesting to note that your father or whoever, is in trouble, for not keeping you under lock and key. The devil will torture him. Do you understand why you receive ice-cold inhuman stares from certain people? Spiritual authority and their skin are on the line. In intense cases, when you dominate, the other person who was being used by the devil dies. Perform or die. That is the devil's motto. Demons are not dull.

But you can be dull if you start regarding your father or whosoever as your enemy. The devil is your enemy. Love people.

Matthew 5:44 *But I say unto you, Love your enemies, bless them that curse you, do good to them that hate you, and pray for them which despitefully use you, and persecute you* [45] *That ye may be the children of your Father which is in heaven: for he maketh his sun to rise on the evil and on the good, and sendeth rain on the just and on the unjust* [46] *For if ye love them which love you, what reward have ye? do not even the publicans the same?*

Bless them that persecute you. Hmm. The word bless is the word **eulogy. You eulogize those who persecute you?** Friend, now you know Christianity is not for the normal. Congratulations. To 'eulogize' is to speak highly of someone. And that is not the only thing you do. Read on. Did the Lord Jesus mean that? Yes He did, He would not have said it if He did not mean it. And He demonstrated it on the cross. Refuse to live in bitterness.

Preacher, you are just doing your job. I want God Himself to come and tell me.

I see you spending more time in the wilderness than 40 years. You are just about to break the record.

So I just leave them?

No.

Then what do I do pastor?

Bless them. Sincerely desire to see good in their lives. We are now talking 'Post Graduate Levels'. When did you last pray for your enemies? Not praying against them, but for them. Listen. The problem is with your understanding. They are called your enemies not from your point of view, but from theirs. They are the ones who regard you as an enemy, not you. You have no enemy apart from the devil and demons.

Be careful with the desire to see God's judgement on others. Going around flashing curses is a dangerous habit. I am pretty sure those in the kingdom of darkness are excited. That's the gospel they want to hear. *Yes. Love us. Love us.* **Wait for the conclusion.** Bitterness and spiritual warfare don't mix. Do not just pick what you feel like picking in the Bible, take the whole package, even that which sounds bitter. Go for the whole Counsel of God. That is growth. **Ours is a unique lifestyle let us demonstrate it and leave vengeance to Him.** In the devil's kingdom, they have been taught how to frustrate and make Christians lose focus. Bitterness is one sure way of conceding defeat. Some people will provoke you deliberately so that you become constantly grieved. As long as you move in bitterness, your spiritual position is being weakened. When you just become born again, you may see traces or effects of the old demonic covenant. You are at a point in life when one covenant is being enforced and the other being revoked. It is here where Christians start wondering whether a curse can work in a believer's life. That curse or effect you see is a result of your not enforcing the new covenant.

Christian understanding of who one is, increases as we move on in our walk. Our understanding of truth grows. *Well, for some.* The more you realize what is really yours and who you are the devil changes his address. But as long as one is ignorant the devil will operate illegally. And what a pretender he is. What are we saying in other words? When a Christian is young, the devil can play hide and seek. When he or she matures, the Christian will put the enemy to flight 24/7. Let us understand something here. **Why I believe a curse is not supposed to work in your life as a mature Christian.**

I. THE ISSUE OF CURSES

A. CURSES

A closer look at the definition of a 'curse' will make Christians pinch themselves for fearing. Jesus rendered the devil ineffective. Keep that in mind. What is a curse?

- ✓ **A <u>Prayer</u> of a wicked man to a demon.** Yes, a curse is a prayer to a demon! Now this is the point I bring you home.

> James 5:16b *... The prayer of a righteous man is powerful and effective.* (NIV)

Did you see that? The prayer of the **wicked** is powerful?! No. **The prayer of a righteous man.** Every born again person is righteous. And your prayer is **both** powerful and effective.

But pastor, my prayers are hitting the ceiling and coming back.

Dear wise Christian, does God live outside your ceiling? **Are you on drugs?** There is too much power in your prayer to blast your ceiling into outer space! If you want your prayers to go that far. As for me, Emmanuel (God with me) is ever present. We have fellowship. Your prayers are powerful and you are righteous!

> Romans 3:21 *But now the righteousness of God without the law is manifested, being witnessed by the law and the prophets;* ²² *Even the righteousness of God which is by faith of Jesus Christ unto all and upon all them that believe: for there is no difference*

God's righteousness is by faith **unto all** and **upon all that believe**. Believe in what? Themselves? Those who think positively? No, positive thinking that does not depend on faith in Jesus is useless and mere New Age philosophy. The Word of God is clear. Believe in Jesus. How plainer should it be before we grasp it?

> Romans 5:17 *For if by one man's offence death reigned by one; much more they which receive abundance of grace and of the gift of righteousness shall reign in life by one, Jesus Christ.)* ¹⁹ *For as by one man's Disobedience many were made sinners, so by the obedience of one shall many be made righteous.*

Righteousness is a gift. So if you do not have it, you have not bothered to collect it. It is free. You have the right to accept or reject a gift. May you do the most sensible thing today and acknowledge that you are righteous. The devil does not want you to know this. He wants you to look for your own righteousness. Friend that is one shortcut to a messed up life. True righteousness cannot be worked for, it can only be received.

> Isaiah 64:6a *But we are all as an unclean thing, and all our righteousnesses are as filthy rags…*

Now get this great secret. Having abandoned our 'righteousness' and accepted His gift, we come to realize that **every child of God's prayer is superior to a wicked person's prayer.** The devil does not want you to even whisper this, lest one of his prisoners over hears it. Whoever is born from above is superior to the one born from below. That is a very important spiritual law in John 3:31 and 15:19. Your prayer is more powerful and more effective than you have ever imagined. Grow up. **When the wicked pray and the righteous pray and the prayers of these two people collide, there is only one direction or outcome, the righteous' way!** Get this. It is very important! The spiritual power of the righteous' prayer overrides the wicked man's prayer. *Take a break to think about this before you come to the second meaning of a curse.*

✓ **A curse is a call or declaration (confession)** for a particular demon to attack someone or something. What does the Word of God say about God's child, the devil's child and the use of words?

Ecclesiastes 8:4a *...a king's word is supreme...* (NIV)

Your word is supreme. Your word is superior to the wicked person's word. Do not fear them.

Psalm 10:7 *His mouth is full of cursing and deceit and fraud: under his tongue is mischief and vanity.*

[8] *He sitteth in the lurking places of the villages: in the secret places doth he murder the innocent: his eyes are privily set against the poor.*

[10] *He croucheth, and humbleth himself, that the poor may fall by his strong ones.*

The wicked are always cursing the righteous. Look at the next verse. **In the secret places**. Friend, the occult is real and many who are ignorant are being murdered through the curses that are unleashed against them! The poor falls by what? Verse ten. His strong ones. The wicked person's strong ones. **Who are these strong ones?** The demons they call upon in their incantations. **Stand up God's child!** When the wicked declare something and you a king and a priest you declare, there is a big difference. Your word is supreme. You are royalty. A peculiar person. That means you are extraordinary. You are uncommon.

1 Peter 2:9a *But ye are a chosen generation, a royal priesthood,*
an holy nation, a peculiar people; that ye should show
forth the praises of him who hath called
you out of darkness into his
marvellous light...

Your declaration is superior! Your word is final, it is supreme. Believe it or not curses are prayers or declarations of the wicked. If the wicked are praying to devils, what are you doing, snoring? **Get up pray and decree in the name of Jesus!!!** And how they flee for their lives! If the curses they were trying to cast upon you fall on them, they deserve it! Now the wicked are getting worried. There are certain people that are determined to destroy you no matter how much love you show them. If you have loved them, sincerely you can boldly say whatever comes upon them, is their fault. You have done all you could and God is your witness. Quote the scriptures below.

Proverbs 26:27 *Whoso diggeth a pit shall fall*
therein: and he that rolleth a stone, it
*will **return** upon him.*

Psalm 10:2 *The wicked in his pride doth persecute*
the poor: let them be taken in the devices
that they have imagined.

Stand on the scriptures and declare. They will eat that which they have been brewing for others. That is very biblical. Decree! Christians are not sissies. **Hit back!**

Pastor, are you saying Christians *can* hit back?

No, dear. You misunderstood me. I am saying, Christians **MUST HIT BACK!**

Who is in-charge? You are. Who holds the sword of the Spirit? You do. Then exercise your authority.

Romans 13:4 *For he is the servant of God to you for good. But if you do evil, have fear; for the sword is not in his hand for nothing: he is God's servant, making God's punishment come on the evil-doer.*

(BBE)

The evil doers are the ones who must fear! I love this scripture. Some people have said it is evil to hit back. We wrestle not against flesh and blood. Let's not fight the people but demons. I agree. *But where are those demons, dear educationist?* Sorcerers and all those in the kingdom of darkness are closely knit with demons. Touch one, you have touched the other! When you hit the demons, you hit the carrier of demons! It is that simple! Come on. We know the operations of the kingdom of darkness. You can't fool us. You just want us to let demons operate freely. There is an abnormal intimacy between the wicked and demons. That is copied from us. When people insult Jesus, will I sit down? Unless he is not my Lord!!! When people attack me unnecessarily, will Jesus sit back? He says whoever touches you touches the apple of my eye! **The scripture above says the sword is not in your hands for nothing!** Those who do evil must fear! Without exercising the authority, the sword is in your hands for nothing. And you will be held accountable.

But pastor Keyworth this is talking about authority.

And you are not authority dear? God is talking about ministers of God! Are you a minister?

But Pastor Keyworth, this is talking about presidents.

Thank you for making it easier for me. Yes this is a common scripture that is universally accepted as referring to government leaders, especially presidents. True. But there is something we need to understand. **What many people do not know is that presidents occupy pastoral positions. They are pastors!**

Huh? The word **minister** or **servant** (of God) in Romans 13:4 means **PASTOR**! (Just as there are true pastors, there are false pastors too). This is also the position of deacons. What are the qualifications of deacons? Go to the book of Acts and you could start with Stephen. This must help some of my fellow pastors who want to give false pieces of advice to presidents in order to appease. How could you lie to a fellow pastor? And with a straight face! Shame.

Colossians 3:9 *Lie not one to another, seeing that ye have put off the old man with his deeds*

And shame on those presidents who hate pastors. They just hate themselves! Congratulations. Now you know the position you occupy is important ministers of God. Now you know you are in charge. Did you see Proverbs 26:27? Decree '**Father the Bible says whoever rolls a stone it will return upon him. I decree that this be the case for anyone who has set himself against me, in the name of Jesus!**' Mean every letter in that sentence! The end times Church is not a weeping church. We are not leaving this place a defeated and dejected army. When the Lord appears, He is coming to take a victorious army, a fearless army that has not cowered before the enemy. When God ruptures the Church, the enemy will be glad we are gone. Why? Because of our fire power!

Psalm 105:38 *Egypt was glad when they were gone, for they feared them greatly.*
(NLT)

Blessed be our God who has not left us to ignorance. We are balanced Christians. Our God is a just God. He won't allow the wicked to push us around. Get scripture and speak it. Use the authority Jesus has given you! Whoever is playing with you is in trouble! Take this scripture for example and begin to speak aloud. This is highly highly feared in satanism, especially if you know who you are in the Lord and you have faith in His Word. Combine at times with fasting. I assure you, the devil's own will fear to whisper your name!

^{Psalm 35:4} *Let those be put to shame and brought to dishonor Who seek after my life; Let those be turned back and brought to confusion Who plot my hurt. ⁵ Let them be like chaff before the wind, And let the angel of the LORD chase them. ⁶ Let their way be dark and slippery, And let the angel of the LORD pursue them. ⁷ For without cause they have hidden their net for me in a pit, Which they have dug without cause for my life. ⁸ Let destruction come upon him unexpectedly, And let his net that he has hidden catch himself; Into that very destruction let him fall.*
(NKJV)

Begin to show forth His praises as you take your position. Remember 1 Peter 2:9? Look at it critically. When you become born again, you become **a Chosen Generation. There is no generational curse in the Chosen Generation**!!! Curses are for the unregenerate. You are born of God. The blood line of curses ended with the old self.

The only way the old self could not transfer its wicked ways is by it dying. **If the old self is dead, there is no way the curses that were upon it could come to you. Impossible!** Romans 6:6. Do not settle for the devil's psychology. Don't fall for his schemes. **If God has blessed you, nobody can curse you**. Numbers 23:20. Nobody. So, no matter what you are facing, maintain what the Bible says about

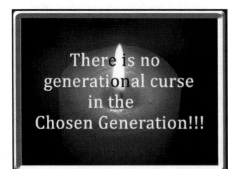

your situation. Your confession will come to pass. It will. It's a must, it will. When somebody asks you about Generational curses, find out which generation they are referring to. Is it the first Adam or the last Adam? If it is the first Adam, yes it's possible. But the last Adam's Generation doesn't have that! Why? You are hid in God. In Christ you live and move and have your being. The curse has to first destroy Jesus before it destroys you! Once Jesus is defeated, then it comes and destroys you. Don't forget, a curse is a demon in operation. If demons can't defeat Jesus, then the devil's psychology got the better of you! **I shall never leave you nor forsake you**. Remember those words? **There is no insurance like that!!!!!!!!**

But pastor Keyworth I have seen people who are saved facing the same curses like before. These curses or situations were there and even after getting saved they have followed them. What do you say?

Dear what I say does not matter, what matters is what the Bible says. When you are born again you are justified. You have no problem before God. When you are born again not only are you justified, you are hid in God. And when you are born again you are not born as an adult but as a babe. A babe the Bible confirms can have 'problems' until it reaches a responsible age. It is only a mature person the Bible calls an ambassador. There is a certain level of maturity expected of ambassadors. If an ambassador is engaged in shameful activities, the governments don't waste time in recalling them. *Does that explain why certain promising men and women pass on before their time? Does God recall them?* It must also be noted that when you become born again the devil would like you to live by sight—the physical senses. When he tells you to live by the physical senses he is saying you are not yet saved, you are from the first Adam. But you are not from the first, you are from the second. So when he fails, he wants to convince you with something Christians fail to see in the Word.

2Thessalonians 2:9 *Even him, whose coming is after*

the working of Satan with all power
and signs and lying
wonders

What you have been experiencing dear are called **lying wonders!** Christians will experience 'curses' to wear them out. Resist the attacks and you have got your 'breakthrough.' Let me show you something and I pray it will open your eyes and answer this puzzle

I have seen people who are saved facing the same curses like before. These curses or situations were there and even after getting saved they have followed them. What do you say Pastor?

Ready? Read the whole chapter of Matthew 14.

Matthew 14:28 *And Peter answered Him and said, "Lord, if it is You, command me to come to You on the water." 29 So He said, "Come." And when Peter had come down out of the boat, he walked on the water to go to Jesus. 30 But when he saw that the wind was boisterous, he was afraid; and beginning to sink he cried out, saying, "Lord, save me!" 31 And immediately Jesus stretched out His hand and caught him, and said to him, "O you of little faith, why did you doubt?"*

Before Jesus appeared on the scene, what was the disciples' problem? The wind and the waves. After Jesus had come, what was Peter's problem? The wind and the waves. But the thing that perplexed me is the strength of the wind and size of the waves as Peter approached Jesus. They seemed to intensify. **Didn't the wind and waves acknowledge the presence of the Creator of the universe?** *Doesn't that curse know you are born again?* And why didn't Jesus do **something**?! Why didn't Jesus rebuke the wind and waves? **The problem was not the wind or the waves. It was**

SATAN'S BEST KEPT SECRETS

the faith of Peter. When he stopped fearing, the wind and waves behaved! Is your faith alright? **Then let the wind and waves in your life behave in the name of Jesus! Don't fall for the devil's lies, switch on your faith and switch off fear! Halleluiah! The wind and the waves are subject to your faith!** Did I mention to you Love, that there are departments in Religion, Science and Philosophy for the sole development of deception? *Pastor Keyworth, what are you saying?* Isis has made sure secret societies develop advanced ways of deceiving people using religion, science and philosophy! Are you a victim?

Being a demon, Isis does not leave out sorcery. For that is the true religion of the underworld. What you have experienced are lying wonders, not real. Those 'curses' are a subterfuge! Pray and maintain your faith in God's Word. Don't you ever settle for lies. When you are born again the blood of Jesus cleanses you from all sin! And it offers protection. Plead the blood upon your life! No devil dare touches you. There is a Passover! The blood is powerful. When satanists sacrifice humans, they expect Satan and demons to honour this covenant by responding to the shed blood. **Do you think the Father will not respond to the greatest sacrifice, the Lord Jesus? His blood is the most powerful. The New Testament is the most powerful agreement in the universe! Hey, use the blood of Jesus NOW! This is the biggest secret Satan doesn't want Christians to know. No sacrifice was, is and will ever equal the sacrifice of Jesus.** Revelation 12:11. Meditate on the Word and declare. The prophets of Old were so tuned to God that they would say, 'So shall it be according to my word!' But you son or daughter of God are closer to Him than all those people were. What is keeping you out of the inheritance? Do not mind the distance, or the deadness of the situation. God's Word travels

^{Psalm 147:15b} *...his word runs swiftly* (NIV).

The Word runs speedily.

193

2 Thessalonians 3:1 *Finally, brethren, pray for us, that the word*
of the Lord may run swiftly and be glorified,
just as it is with you
(NKJV)

When you speak it goes to the target, like a computer guided missile. Be specific in your declarations! Where it finds death it brings life

John 6:63 *The Spirit gives life; the flesh counts for nothing.*
The words I have spoken to you are spirit
and they are life. (NIV)

Where the human efforts cannot help, it enters and changes.

Hebrews 4:12 *For the word of God is living and active. Sharper*
than any double-edged sword, it penetrates even
to dividing soul and spirit, joints
and marrow... (NIV).

Where sin has been or disease, the Word of God dominates.

Acts 19:20 *So mightily grew the word of*
God and prevailed.

The Word prevails, that is its character. Read Numbers 23:23 and Luke 10:19, remember our discussion? Go back to it. Put side by side the two covenants—the curse and the Blessing are incomparable. The Blessing far outweighs the curse in power. But it is the enforcing that makes the difference. **The most enforced is the most effective.** Prayer is enforcing the covenant. Some people cry and cry. *Why Jesus are you doing nothing?* Dig in your heels. Pray and pray in faith. It is you who is doing nothing. Some people turn to fasting as a gimmick to get quick answers. It does not happen that way. As long as you have not been leading a prayerful life, a quickie will not do the job. You will just starve.

Be disciplined. The word disciple and discipline go hand in hand. Are you Jesus' disciple? Then be disciplined.

As for the declarations, come on Rookie, get up! The devil is a master of psychology. He wins most of the battles through psychology. I remember a time I was praying in 1996. Things were tough. The more I prayed the more things went wrong. I told God, 'I'm tired. You are doing nothing to help me.' I got on my bed. I wasn't on that bed for more than 60 seconds i.e. 1 minute. A voice thundered, **'Get up and fight!'** That destroyed all the theology I knew. Jesus, I was taught, speaks in a small gentle voice. What I heard was the opposite. A Commander. And He never sounded like one who was going to tone down His order. As I landed on my knees, I was complaining that Jesus was cruel. *We have been babies in nappies before.*

But a minute in my prayer the Holy Ghost took over. The Lord said, 'This is what is happening'. He gave me a vision: I saw myself in a fight with another person. As we were fighting this person seemed to smile. In fact, the smile was constant. I punched hard, but the smile was still there. Not even flinching! I punched with brute force. The smile was still there. I became discouraged. Then I saw a big hand reach for the face of that other person and peel the face off! **It was a mask!** And just there I saw the most discouraged being. I was made to get his thoughts; **Why is this one not giving up?** *So, that's what the devil was thinking about me, huh?* From that day, I do not give up.

Come what may or may what come. I have spiritual insight. Friend, I'm not someone to encourage like that. I behave like a shark that has scented blood. I got totally nuts. Have you ever been fed-up of being a punching bag? I wish you knew what I'm talking about. Five days later, I got my answer. You may just be 5 days from your solution. Don't stop praying. **God answers prayer that has your heart into it.** Mean it. **If you are discouraged learn one thing from this, the devil is in a worse state!** He is more discouraged than you are! **Believe it or not, most of the times when you reach the point of discouragement, the devil is in a worse state.** Don't you ever forget this spiritual secret.

That vision does not only apply to Keyworth, it applies to you. You and me are family. We are branches. There is nothing special about me that does not apply to you. I do not believe God made me see that for personal benefit. God knew, you and me would meet, not in person maybe, but through this message. He knew what you would need today. Receive the Word that changes all your future. Never be discouraged. It's a trick. Congratulations. You have graduated. **No more discouragement.** The only discouragement you know from now, is the one you dispense to the devil and his wicked ones. Dispense it with joy.

Come on! Start making those declarations. Breathe fire! Speak scripture. As you speak, know it is done. It is impossible for it not to be done. The worst thing I have seen among the believers is that they want someone else to do all the donkey-work while they wallow in the mud like pigs. Spiritual declarations are a lifestyle. Friend it is DIY. **Do it yourself!**

Do you know that there is a Generational Anointing flowing that you must recognize? The devil has made sure Christians talk only about the curse. Christians must seriously ask for forgiveness for glorifying the devil. Am I dramatizing and down playing Satan? I wish. I know Old Nick has '*power*'. He is no pushover. But if you know who you are and whose you are, Old Nick knows he is no match. He is yes pushover!!! But glorifying him, 'The devil has done this, the devil has done that'. That is nonsense. We have a Generational Blessing at work. It is available to any human being! Even those who are not yet born it is waiting for them.

II. THE ISSUE OF THE ULTIMATE BLESSING

'Arise, shine' many Christians have been told, but they seem not to understand. It is impossible to arise with scanty knowledge and understanding. Saints want to arise, but seem to lack the details. Some spend all their lives in seminars and conferences. The result? *To be blessed.* That is the poorest vision I have ever heard! Even witches do not have it. As a king, the first territory of leadership is your family. The second is your neighborhood. That is what the Bible says. You are blessed to bless. Think beyond self all the time. Witches and wizards always think of how to impact their society and the nations, why should Christians have such poor and very short sighted ideas? You are being equipped to equip. Paul, Peter, John, Timothy and Priscilla are not coming back. And we do not need them. But we need you. You are our Paul, Peter, John, Timothy and Priscilla. *You really mean that pastor?* You mean you didn't know? God is counting on you to take the Gospel wherever you are or live. At the market, in the shop, in the work place. Organize seminars and spiritual talks and call pastors where it is necessary, otherwise, you teach what you have been taught. *Pastor Keyworth, are you talking to me?* No, I am talking to Adolf Hitler. Ephesians 4:11-12. The pastor's work is to train you so that you go and do ministry. *Huh?* Read your Bible. Now that you are ready to go, do you need something? Yes.

Before you arise, shine according to Isaiah 60:1, let me take you a step back. This is one step, though backwards, that takes you many steps forward. **This is one of the ultimate secrets!** The devil doesn't want you to know this. In fact the devil has stolen this from many Christians. I pray you are not one of them. Go through this secret every day. Understand it. No devil will like you. The wicked will scamper!

Isaiah 59:21 *As for me, this is my covenant with them, saith the LORD; My spirit that is upon thee, and my words which I have put in thy mouth, shall not depart out of thy mouth, nor out of the mouth of thy seed, nor out of the mouth of thy seed's seed, saith the LORD, from henceforth and forever.* 60:1 *Arise, shine; for thy light is come, and the glory of the LORD is risen upon thee.*

Let's get back to kindergarten. We ask a few questions.

✓ **Who is speaking?**

✓ **To whom is He speaking?**

- ✓ **Who are 'them'?**

- ✓ **What does the 'Spirit of the Lord upon' mean?**

- ✓ **What is 'the word in the mouth'?**

These five questions will revolutionize your life. You will understand why it is treason of the highest degree not to arise and shine! **The whole satanic system is based on destroying this secret. And the counterfeit rewards of power and dominion in the kingdom of darkness are all based on this! And this is the reason why getting into the occult is the worst kind of demotion!!!**

THE EXPLANATION

- ✓ Friend, we are behind the curtains, in The Boardroom of the Godhead The Father, The Son and The Holy Spirit. The meeting is in progress. Let us eaves drop. Shh. Keep quiet. **God the Father is speaking...**

- ✓ **He is talking to Jesus.** The Messiah. The Redeemer. The Arm of the LORD.

- ✓ **'Them'** are actually the spiritual children, the disciples of Jesus and the disciples' disciples etc. That means **you** and **me**. What are they planning for us? This is a covenant. **Generational covenant**. It will pass from generation to generation. Jesus is the Head of the family. Heb. 2:13

- ✓ **The Anointing upon Jesus will run through the family from generation to generation.** I now understand what the scriptures say in 1 Peter 2:9 we are a **Chosen Generation**, a generation of exploits, special people, not ordinary. I have always refused to be an ordinary person. This confirms it. When you are in Christ, you are chosen. I don't know if I won't be caught now. I feel like shouting! **HALLELUIAH!!! Wow.**

✓ The **'word in your mouth'** is the Gospel of Jesus, John 14:24. The Word of faith we preach. **It is also the Authority that comes from knowing who you are in the Lord.** The power to decree comes from this!

When I speak it is like Jesus has spoken the Word?

Yes, Billy.

I'm evicting the devils today!

Go for it my brother, evict them.

Oh I'm screaming now! I feel like Brother Billy. The Bible mentions three things regarding the Holy Spirit.

✓ The Holy Spirit shall be in you—The Seal (Ownership), John 14:17

✓ The Holy Spirit shall be with you—The Security and Guidance, John 14:17

✓ The Holy Spirit shall be upon you—The Service, Acts 1:8

When the Holy Spirit is upon you, dominion is your life. The devil cannot push you around. Yokes of bondage are destroyed. Let's look at this scripture's confirmation from the New Testament.

Mark 16:15 *He said to them, "Go into all the world and preach the good news to all creation. :16 Whoever believes and is baptized will be saved, but whoever does not believe will be condemned. :17 And these signs will accompany those who believe: In my name they will drive out demons; they will speak in new tongues; :18 they will pick up snakes with their hands; and when they drink deadly poison, it will not hurt them at all; they will place their hands on sick people, and they will get well." :19 After the Lord Jesus had spoken to them, he was taken up into heaven and he sat at the right hand of God. :20 Then*

the disciples went out and preached everywhere,
and the Lord worked with them and confirmed
his word by the signs that
accompanied it.

Common sense shows there are two ways of looking at this scripture, the **Traditional** and the **Biblical**. In the traditional approach, we say God was performing miracles in the lives of the disciples as they preached the Word. The disciples cast out devils, they spoke with new tongues, they laid hands on the sick and the sick recovered. Hooray. This is not the total truth. That is not what the Bible is REALLY saying. Sometimes we imagine things into the Bible. **Who is teaching us the Bible?** A very important revelation has been given to us and we have swept it under the carpet. This is one secret the devil does not want you to know. When I first saw it, shock and joy fell on me. Let's look at this scripture critically.

- ✓ **Verse 15:** Jesus is talking to the disciples, that is straight forward. We do not need an African Union meeting over this.

- ✓ **Verse 16:** Jesus is telling the disciples that anyone who believes the Gospel they preach will be saved and who-ever does not will be condemned. Clear.

- ✓ **Verse 17:** Jesus is now explaining the kind of life the ones who believe are going to display. When they accept the gospel their lives will become **supernatural.**

¹⁷ *And these signs will accompany*
those who believe
(Emphasis added)

Jesus does not mean the original disciples, NO NO NO! The key verse becomes verse 17! Jesus is telling the disciples that **those** who believe in the message they preach and are baptized will be saved. But not only that. There is more that accompanies salvation. The Bible is clear about this in Hebrews 6:9. Jesus continues by saying **those** who believe will have the ability to cast out devils and perform wonders. He is talking about the disciples' disciples! And this trend is a continuous process. This is what Isaiah 59:21 is talking about. **The INVINCIBILITY OF THE CHURCH throughout all generations! I am excited! We are as bold as lions! Divine power flows through us. Not an imitation.** But verse 20 of Mark 16, what does it say? **God confirmed.** How? **What Jesus told the disciples would happen to the new believers is what was confirmed!** Of course there is an element of the sick recovering and all that when the disciples laid hands, but that is not what God was putting across here. **It is the transference of the kingdom life, power and authority in the word and all blessings, without a single curse from one generation of believers to another! Don't take this lightly. Your life may depend on it.** *But pastor Keyworth miracles ended a long time ago.*

Correct. I agree with you. I even have the proof. Miracles ended the day God the Father died. I attended His funeral. Since He was unpopular only a few of us attended. We are really saddened by the loss of the Great One. Great condolences to all Christians. May He rest in peace. **Friend, tradition is killing us. The anointing is supernatural! The anointing of Jesus is from one generation to another! God the Father promised it! If God the Father is dead so are miracles! IF NOT stop wishful sinking or is it thinking? We have supernatural ignorance today in the Church because**

- ✓ As long as our spiritual forefathers did not mention something then it is false. Ignorance is running in the family.
- ✓ The devil is teaching us and we are merry.
- ✓ We do not like the people God has used to bring out a particular truth.
- ✓ We refuse to seriously study with the Spirit of God guiding us.

And do you know what it means to cast out devils in His name? It means authority over the source of all problems. Most problems have the spirit world, the kingdom of darkness as their source. Those so-called curses are demonic stunts. Cast them out! Jesus is saying you don't have to ask me for help all the time. **Simply recognize the presence of the Holy Spirit upon you! From today your path is clear.**

CAST THE DEMONS OUT! And if you can cast demons out, you can cast curses out! Since they are the same thing! Kindergarten common sense. Casting devils out is a miracle. Divine ability is yours now.

> 2 Peter 1:3 *According as his divine power hath given unto us all things that pertain unto life and godliness, through the knowledge of him that hath called us to glory and virtue* [4] ***Whereby are given unto us exceeding great and precious promises: that by these ye might be partakers of the divine nature,*** *having escaped the corruption that is in the world through lust.*
>
> (Emphasis added)

By the promises you might be a partaker of the divine nature. Friend the answer is in the promises. The word 'might' shows that you can either receive this or reject it. Jesus promises that their hands (new believers) are charged with the cure for any disease or ailment. This is the biblical life for anyone who believes in Jesus. Do you remember Hebrews 2:13? What does it say?

> *And again: "I will put My trust in Him." And again: "Here am I and the children whom God has given Me."*
>
> (NKJV)

Who is speaking? Jesus! But this scripture is not complete. Let's look at it in full. Let's get the full message of our Lord Jesus.

> Isaiah 8:18 *Here am I and the children whom the LORD has given*
> *me! We are for signs and wonders in Israel*
> *From the LORD of hosts, Who*
> *dwells in Mount Zion.*
> (NKJV)

The Bible is sweet! **WE ARE FOR SIGNS AND WONDERS! JESUS HAS SAID IT! I feel like dancing now!!! Jesus is my Saviour and He is my Lord. He owns everything about me. He owns me. Totally. Shame on the partial believers.** Many want Jesus to be their Savior but not Lord. He cannot be one and not the other. It ain't gonna happen. Jesus is our Savior, He has saved us. But He is Lord too. As Savior, He has given us a unique position, He has made us perfect. Yes, you are perfect.

> Hebrews 10:14 *because by one sacrifice he has made perfect*
> *forever those who are being made holy. ¹⁵ᵃ The*
> *Holy Spirit also testifies to*
> *us about this.*

Christians do not know this. This is a Christian's Positional Truth. On the other side is the Practical Truth. Your walk in this life has to be perfected, it is not yet perfect. While everyone has the same Positional level, the walk differs. It is this that needs improving on. Each individual Christian has a responsibility to see that their walk is improving for this makes their light to shine brighter in this pitch-dark world. Jesus as Lord desires this, for it shows your godly reverence for Him. Every Lord expects to be respected and His word honored. One whose Lord is Jesus does not willingly dash for sin. He refuses to give in to it, and if he stumbles, he asks for forgiveness immediately.

III. THE ISSUE OF ANOTHER WAY

Christians want Jesus to remove their sins and guilt then they go back to their sinning ways, like a dog going back to its vomit. Today, sin is not talked about, in some places, because it is 'attacking' the brethren. The presentation I agree matters, but to just say people will change without giving help and direction is gross irresponsibility. The ministerial offices are to help the saints. Being born again is not a license to evil. The New Testament, not the Old, is very aggressive on the issue of sin. The Bible says there are three sins in the New Testament.

> Hebrews 10:29 *How much more severely do you think a man deserves to be punished who has trampled the Son of God under foot, who has treated as an unholy thing the blood of the covenant that sanctified him, and who has insulted the Spirit of grace?* (NIV)

To whom is this scripture talking, to the unbelievers or to the believers? Have you seen the deadly three?

✓ Trampling the Son of God

A person who just excites himself that Jesus is his Savior but ignores the fact that He is Lord, is treading on thin ice. Jesus as Lord takes first place in a Christian's life. We have no life of our own, anymore. Your old nature that did as it pleased died a long time ago. For you to live is Christ. That is what God's Word says. The body is not mine. I own nothing. I am just a steward. In the parable of the evil servants, the Lord of the vineyard came to destroy the servants because they were denying Him access to his vineyard. They took it as their personal possession. Do not make the same fatal mistake.

And this is the folly of all those who are saying Jesus is not the Only Way. They are trampling on the Son of God. If Jesus is not the Only Way, which other way is there? Tell us. Shame! You think pleasing man or the devil will save you?

✓ Treating as unholy the Blood

Anyone who refuses to recognize the blood of Jesus not only insults God's mercies, but also defies the consequences of this action. This is one of the highest forms of pride. One clearly places himself or herself in a position of self-righteous and holiness. He refuses to realize that judgement has to fall on anything that is not covered in the blood. Such a one says, 'Let judgment come upon me we see'. Today people do not believe God judges sin, and they are daring Him. The Church is leading the procession. That's why they are saying Jesus is not the answer. They take His blood lightly. A few years back I heard two people arguing. One was saying God is sending judgment on America if we continue living carelessly. The other furiously countered, 'God can't judge America! It's a great nation!' What an unwise thing to say! God will judge nations small and great. Rich or poor. Greatness won't keep America. If America is wicked then judgment falls. If Zambia is wicked, God won't look at its per capita, but on His own, those who fear Him and are covered in the Blood of Jesus. They are the ones the Lord will protect. So let us not fool ourselves with false peace. 1 Thessalonians 5:3. Let's respect the true owner of life. Judgment will fall whether you believe it or not and the worst part? The longer judgment is delayed the more severe it will be.

> Ecclesiastes 8:11 *Because sentence against an evil work*
> *is not executed speedily, therefore the heart*
> *of the sons of men is fully set*
> *in them to do evil.*

Just because someone did it, I-can-also-do-it syndrome is spreading like wildfire. Good. Do it. Evil will be judged, it doesn't matter how long it takes. The Bible is clear, God will judge nations, presidents, people and He will start with the Church. Psalm 9:8, Isaiah 3:14 and

> 1Peter 4:17 *For the time is come that judgment must begin at the house of God: and if it first begin at us, what shall the end be of them that obey not the gospel of God? ¹⁸ And if the righteous scarcely be saved, where shall the ungodly and the sinner appear?*

> Ecclesiastes 12:14 *For God shall bring every work into judgment, with every secret thing, whether it be good, or whether it be evil.*

✓ Totally insulting the Spirit of Grace

Christ was not happy with the Pharisees because even when they knew that He was using the power of the Holy Spirit, they called it demonic power. The opposite has just taken place in our times. With full knowledge of a particular work, that it is the working of demons, we still audaciously ascribe it to the Holy Spirit, just because we are desperate for a miracle. It is the same sin, but on the flipside. Not only that, Christians today are doing every evil thing that the world is doing in the name of grace. Lady Grace has been abused. The things that are being done in the name of grace are appalling. Understand me; I do not claim to be perfect in my walk with God. I am striving. And as I strive I urge you, because you are my beloved, that we strive together and do not miss it, we have come a long way. We cannot just lose heart now. Even as people flavor the Gospel for personal gain, let us know how to serve our King with godly fear, if we really believe He is coming. Our greatest and only blessings are found in Christ. By the way, have you noticed that the scripture Hebrews 10: 29 is a question demanding an answer from you? Answer it.

> Hebrews 10:26 *For if we sin wilfully after that we have received the knowledge of the truth, there remaineth*

no more sacrifice for sins, ^{27} But a certain
fearful looking for of judgment and
fiery indignation, which
shall devour the
adversaries.

Child of the Most High, God's blessings are not enjoyed outside His presence. The world is trying to force us to do just that. The prodigal son came face to face with this reality. He returned to his father. God's blessings cannot be enjoyed outside Jesus. Do not regard the gift more than the giver. It is idolatry. Once you have the right stance the devil is no match. Satan *'has power'*. However, the greatest difference between Satan and God is that while Satan *has some power* God is The Power!

Matthew 26:64 *Jesus said to him, "It is as you said.*
Nevertheless, I say to you, hereafter you will
see the Son of Man sitting at the right
hand of the Power, and coming
on the clouds of heaven."
(NKJV)

And this power is in you. Oh, I'm grateful to Jesus. Thank you Father. Thank you Holy Spirit. Halleluiah! **The anointing of Jesus runs in me.** This anointing does not border on R.A.G.S. i.e. Race, Age, Gender and Status. All are welcome as long as they are faithful, available and teachable. Are you? It is your time. Now is the time to arise and shine. The only thing that can stop you is not the devil, but your unbelief. Many erroneously think eternal life is only Quantity or longevity of life, no. It also means Quality of life. As you understand this, may Quality be added to your life in the Name of Jesus. When you have understood Isaiah 59:21 then look at the next verse, Isaiah 60:1 God commissions you to Arise, Shine.

Do you know what awaits you? You are destined for miracles. Your life is supernatural. The Bible says not believing this testimony is **insulting God**. What testimony? That we have this supernatural life!

> 1 John 5:10b *Anyone who does not believe God has made him out to be a liar,* [11] *And this is the testimony: God has given us eternal life, and this life is in his Son.*
>
> (Emphasis added)

I stopped doubting God when I saw this scripture. **Unbelief is not just saying 'no' to God. It is insulting Him.** Not believing what He says in the Bible is calling Him a **liar.** The word liar means a **deceiver or falsifier!** What you are saying is that God is the devil. Stop doubting and believe what He says about you. Why do people find it easier to receive the message of death from the devil and resist the message of life from God? David, do you also see the folly of saying Jesus is not the only way to God in 1 John 5:10b? **It is actually not believing the same God they are saying they believe in and not only that, but also calling Him a liar!** It is impossible to be a Christian and say Jesus is not the only way! You are a Christian because you are Jesus Christ like. If Jesus is not the only way, you are not part of Jesus, then how can you be called a Christian, the one you have rejected?

> John 12:48 *But all who reject me and my message will be judged on the day of judgment by the truth I have spoken.* [49] *I don't speak on my own authority. The Father who sent me has commanded me what to say and how to say it.* [50] *And I know his commands lead to eternal life; so I say whatever the Father tells me to say.*
>
> (NLT)

The Father is the one who told Jesus what to say and how to say it! How can the Father start contradicting Himself that He has another way today? Does Jehovah, my Dad, suffer from amnesia? And He has revealed the new ways only to some super stars of preachers? Unless it is another father they are talking about...whose weakest spot you about to find out in the next chapter.

9.

SATAN'S WEAKEST SPOT

Job 20:4 *Do you not know from of old, since the time that man was placed on the earth, ⁵ That the triumphing of the wicked is short, and the joy of the godless and defiled is but for a moment? ⁶ Though his [proud] height mounts up to the heavens and his head reaches to the clouds, ⁷ Yet he will perish forever like his own dung; those who have seen him will say, Where is he? ¹² Though wickedness is sweet in his mouth, though he hides it under his tongue, ¹³ Though he is loath to let it go but keeps it still within his mouth, ¹⁴ Yet his food turns [to poison] in his stomach; it is the venom of asps within him.*

(AMP)

ALL Christians should know another best-kept secret of Satan: **the devil is not only cursed by God, he is The Curse in the fullest sense of the word. Whatever he touches dies. Read on and you will understand.** Jesus is not only blessed, he is The Very Blessing. So when the devil tells someone, 'Come and get a blessing from me,' he is lying. He has no capacity to bless even if he wanted to. Look at this verse.

Proverbs 10:22 *The blessing of the LORD, it maketh rich, and he addeth no sorrow with it.*

I.   SATAN AND THE LIFE OF FAILURE

Here we are given the difference between God's blessing and the devil's. The devil has no capacity to bless. When he does, death is tied to it. Receiver beware. This scripture clearly states that when God blesses there is **no bodily pain, mental torture or even spiritual harm awaiting the receiver**. An ancient wise man once said, 'I fear Greeks when they come with gifts'. He must have mistaken the devil for the Greeks or is it the other way round? Every gift from the devil is fatal. Every. **Remember, the most sincere thing the devil will ever speak, under oath, is a lie.**

> John 8:44b *... there is no truth in him. When he lies, he speaks his native language, for he is a liar and the father of lies.* (NIV)

The Lord Jesus gave us the true nature or character of our enemy. The devil's truth are lies. His native language is lies, lies, lies. And he speaks them with all sincerity. That is how bad it is. He has no more conscience that he is lying, to him that is what is normal. He hates you and will not stop until he destroys you. **He wants you to be a partaker of his cursed nature, NOT a partaker of God's divine nature. 2 Peter 1:4.** This is a well guarded secret. Beware. **The devil capitalizes on the selfishness of people. The devil's power is for selfishness, while God's power is for love. It does not matter whether the one exuding the power is a man of the cloth, as long as that power is from the devil, then it is for selfishness. The ultimate goal is to mislead victims to the devil's side.** Ladies and gentlemen let's open the vault of truth about the devil. Let's see what he really is like. **There is no one in the whole universe who is as cursed as the devil is.** In Genesis 3:14 and Hebrews 2:14 we see that God cursed the devil with **Eternal Failure**. Are you getting this? **Many Christians do not know this. In fact most satanists don't know this either.** This sums up all the devil's nature and efforts. **This is the devil's weakest spot. The secret, he constantly keeps from his own every day. This is the source of all his tirades.** His temper comes from this. **Defeat and failure are his life style.**

Children of God must see this and take advantage. **When the Bible talks about the serpent's head being dealt a death blow and him scratching the Seed's heel, in Genesis 3, those are permanent and temporal blows being talked about.**

Genesis 3:14 And the LORD God said unto the serpent, Because thou hast done this, thou art cursed above all cattle, and above every beast of the field; upon thy belly shalt thou go, and dust shalt thou eat all the days of thy life.*15* And I will put enmity between thee and the woman, and between thy seed and her seed; it shall bruise thy head, and thou shalt bruise his heel.

What does that mean? **The devil will always fail no matter what he does.** Jesus will always succeed no matter how odd the conditions are. The good news is, those trends run through the families.

Proverbs 9:33 *The curse of the LORD is on the house of the wicked, But He blesses the home of the just.*
(NKJV)

The devil and all his children are cursed. The Bible in John 8:44 clearly tells us that although God loves the world (people) it does not make all of them His. Some have a father, the devil. And as long as the devil is their father, they are under this curse that hangs on the devil's house! This curse of failure hangs on the devil. When he was Lucifer, before he fell, the devil had this anointing of not failing. Today, ladies and gentlemen, it is different. **Failure is his lifestyle.** The Lord Jesus mentioned this principle in

> John 16:20 *Verily, verily, I say unto you, That ye shall weep and lament, but the world shall rejoice: and ye shall be sorrowful, but your sorrow shall be turned into joy.*

Your sorrow will be turned into joy! In the following verses He says that joy cannot be stolen or destroyed. **Permanent joy.** And for the devil's pals, their rejoicing will turn into **eternal damnation!** That is the best definition of **short lived joy.** If the devil succeeds in your life, check where you are missing it. **The devil is a failure, and he must do nothing else in your life but fail. Always.** The **worst** thing that could ever happen to you as a Christian is a **temporal** setback. But even that setback has something good about it.

> Romans 8:28 *And we know that all things work together for good to them that love God, to them who are the called according to his purpose.*

And we **know**, not we *believe*. Many are trying to force themselves to believe. Wrong direction. **You must know.** *I believe I am a person.* No. I know and I do not even talk about it.

All things work together for good. Do you know that? It is not for everyone though; it is only for those who **love** God. If you really love God, know all things are going according to God's sweet plan for you. **The best thing that could ever happen to the devil is permanent defeat.** I know you missed that point. Read it again. **When things favor the devil, somewhere somehow he is about to suffer shock!** That is the curse upon his life. Read job 20:6. It says though he appears to have attained great heights, he will perish like his dung!!! Look at how God deals with the whore in Revelation. The one who makes everyone shudder.

Revelation 18:8 *"Therefore her plagues will come in one day——death and mourning and famine. And she will be utterly burned with fire, for strong is the Lord God who judges her*
(NKJV)

In one day! From riches to rags, from feasting to famine! **Whatever the devil touches dies or fails always!** The great scheme that has plagued mankind—the whore has just perished! Ever sat down to watch cartoons? The bad guy will giggle because his nefarious scheme is about to go well and just that moment, KABOOM! It all falls apart. That is the devil's picture, always going wrong at the last moment. When it matters most. *Am sure the devil hates these guys who make cartoons, they remind him what he wishes he could forget.* The destruction that this wicked whore of Revelation has made is devastating!

II. SATAN'S TRADE IN SOULS

Amy I am sure you remember that in Chapter One we mentioned the trade in human parts and touched a little on cloning. Human body parts is big business. This is not debatable. It is common knowledge. We all know what is going on. Witchcraft and the issue of human parts go hand in hand. Time would fail us if we had to talk about the ritual killings in various places of the earth. The hunt for albino blood. The hunt for private parts and the insatiable desire for fetuses all indicate the madness we have succumbed to. Human beings are traded in many ways today. Souls are light things. Every soul that is misled to the devil's side brings great honor to those who did. The spiritual battles we are engaged in are about souls. Many unfortunately are super ignorant. It is painful seeing the way people are tormented and traded through pornography—men and women forced to have sex with animals and to even drink the semen of animals for a trifling sum, drug trafficking—putting drugs in their private parts—it is sickening! Babies sexually molested. Undiluted madness.

Bodies and souls for sale. The porn stars have to be on drugs to try to get by because of the satanic torture they undergo. When the conscience hits them, suicide beckons, the very thing the devil desired in the first place, the destruction of their bodies and souls. Jesus Christ is the answer. Come to Jesus, the devil has nothing to offer. Absolutely nothing! The Bible has mentioned something very interesting which we must do well paying attention to. There is one focal point for all this evil trade. **It reveals the one in charge of all this trade.** Did you know that? All this satanic trade in humans, conjured up wars, human body parts, mind control, misinformation and torture of people converges on one spot. You must know this Satan's best-kept secret. The major buyer of all this, the major beneficiary from all this evil trade is THE GREAT WHORE! Surprised? Every major issue we are going to experience or have experienced has been put down by God in His Holy Word. Read this

> Revelation 18:11 *"And the merchants of the earth will weep and mourn over her, for no one buys their merchandise anymore:*
> *13 ...bodies and souls*
> *of men.*
> (NKJV)

Why are the merchants crying? There is no one to buy their merchandise! Which or what merchandiseWho benefits from all the unnecessary wars we see? The Great Whore. Bodies of men sacrificed. Innocent blood, shed. Libation. The blood seeps into the soil. **Satan receives the sacrifice from the Whore of the Book of Revelation.** Brethren the battle we are engaged in is a battle of the body and the soul. Demons desire bodies to occupy. This is the Host-Parasite Technique. They will do all they can to live in human bodies. And that is also the place the Holy Spirit MUST occupy. These bodies we take lightly are highly valued in the spirit world. Take care of that body. The coming of the Antichrist is to make every human being have demons living in them. And I don't stand to be corrected on this point! But towards the enslaving of the whole world to Satan, the process will see a lot of human bodies being traded in one form or the other. Souls? The Church is the center. Souls are being offered to the devil, when people with eyes wide open refuse to heed what is very visible. When people reject Jesus as the Only Way, and you know your pastor or priest or clergy has the same stance and you are seated under him, your soul is on the devil's altar.

Romans 16:17 *Now, it is my desire, brothers, that you will take note of those who are causing division and trouble among you, quite against the teaching which was given to you: and keep away from them.*
18 For such people are not servants of the Lord Christ, but of their stomachs; and by their smooth and well-said words the hearts of those who have no knowledge of evil are tricked.

(BBE)

Most of the times when you point out wickedness, you become the villain. You are labeled divisive and a trouble maker. But who is causing division and trouble? **The Bible says those who are teaching another gospel!** Those people we respect very much and fall down before, it doesn't matter how we feel about them, THEY ARE NOT Christians if they preach another gospel! This feel-good gospel, sweet-talking people at the expense of truth is highly highly devilish! I have no respect for such. I know where they are leading people. Like my Father I am no respecter of persons. Have you seen the good part of this scripture? **They only trick the ignorant, those who have no knowledge of evil. The immature.** Have you been tricked? Whom do you sit under? Take time to weigh issues. If you entertain this false gospel you have no excuse. **You are no longer Christ's.** You must think about this seriously. If Jesus is not the only way, then

- ✓ The Bible is false.

- ✓ There is no eternal life, in short there is no salvation.

- ✓ There is an alternative to Christianity—Galatians 1:6

- ✓ He is not deity—Micah 5:2, Phil 2:6

- ✓ The first disciples are crooks—Ephesians 3:5, 1 John4:6

- ✓ He is a liar—Hebrews 4:15

- ✓ The Holy Spirit is wicked—1 John 5:6

- ✓ God the Father is a liar—John 5:37

What is eternal life? Is it the sweet all-is-well gospel? That is sensual wisdom. The Bible is clear.

> John 17:3 *"And this is eternal life, that they may know You, the only true God, and Jesus Christ whom You have sent.*
> (NKJV)

If you do not know the only true God and Jesus whom he has sent, you have no idea what eternal life is. Please keep quiet! The claimants of this new gospel acknowledge not being in the Way (Jesus). Hence they are not Christians. How dare you sit under such and claim you are still a Christian! **COME OUT AND SAVE YOUR SOUL. COME OUT!** Or do you love the praise of man more than that of God? Do not lie that you were not told. On this day you have been told. Take it or leave it.

> Jeremiah 7:25 *From the day your ancestors left Egypt until now, I have continued to send my servants, the prophets——day in and day out.* ²⁶ *But my people have not listened to me or even tried to hear. They have been stubborn and sinful——even worse than*

their ancestors. (NLT)

What makes you sit under such clergy is your love for sin and nothing else! Total undiluted rebellion is what is in your blood stream. **And rebellion and witchcraft are equal in the sight of God.**

1 Samuel 15:23 *For rebellion is as the sin of witchcraft, and stubbornness is as iniquity and idolatry. Because thou hast rejected the word of the LORD, he hath also rejected thee from being king.*

So do not be surprised to find you are neighbours with a witch or wizard in hell. In short, you are not different from a witch or wizard. To be specific it means someone rebellious is equal to a witchdoctor or diviner! Clap for yourself, now you know you are a certified witchdoctor.

1 Samuel 15:23 *...Because thou hast rejected the word of the LORD, he hath also rejected thee from being king.*

Those who reject The Word (Jesus), are rejected from being royalty! They are not part of the royal family. Revelation 1:5-6. No matter how nice they look, no matter how sweet they talk, they are not royalty. Are you for Darkness or Light? Come out of rebellion in the name of Jesus! Dear, I know this very very well. The whore of Revelation is in charge of all this satanic subterfuge. False extra-biblical discoveries, conjured up wars, false economic slumps, pornographic industry which makes abnormal revenue-thousands of billions of dollars, experiments with various drugs on people, conjured up diseases, deliberate infection of innocent lives, all evils you know, the whore holds the tether!

But as strange and scary as that may be, the devil has the quality to fail. Not everyone will accept his nonsense. Some whose eyes will be opened, because they are willing, will run and find refuge under the shadow of the Almighty and He will save them. The devil's plan will be shuttered. As painful as some situations may seem, God has a way. Beloved, **when all seems sour, just know you are about to be promoted.**

Nahum 1:3 *The LORD is slow to anger, and great in power,*
and will not at all acquit the wicked: the LORD
hath his way in the whirlwind
and in the storm...

That which seems to have no solution, dear it has a solution. That storm, God has a way to see you through it. There is nothing the devil will ever throw at you that you can't handle. Nothing. Fear and undiluted unbelief are what drives people from God's haven, His word, into the devil's cauldron of wickedness. Friend, there is a way, no matter what it is. Be still and know that he is God and above Him, there is no other.

Brethren in your Christian walk you will encounter stubborn challenges. Problems that seem not to go away. The devil is a master of illusions. Lying wonders. He is defeated but he is trying to trick you. He is playing psychology. Refuse to give in. In such situations go for WAP. WAP in Christianity? *Where else?* How does it work? 'W' for Worship. For stubborn problems worship. You will never go wrong. Worship is the most pure form of prayer because there is no selfishness in it. Worship puts God first. 'A' for Authority that comes from knowing who you are as revealed by scripture. Stand your ground. Order the devil to pack and go. Authority drives out self pity. You cannot have self pity and authority at the same time. And lastly 'P' for Praise. If you lead a life of praise the walls will fall. Praise always insults the situation. It sees the end of the matter, before the end actually appears. No wonder the devil packs quickly. He wants to dampen your spirit, but you actually get jovial and claim your victory! He has no choice but to wet his pants. *Poor mama devil, she has to change his* *diapers constantly.* These three go hand in hand. Unleash them and no walls of evil will stand in your presence.

III. SERIOUS TRAPS FROM ISIS

Christians in general have for a long time been sitting at the devil's feet, and the devil has been pumping devilish doctrine into the Church. Many people who are supposed to be on the move doing exploits for God are stagnant, why? Whenever they try to move someone says, 'God's ways are not your ways, His thoughts are not your thoughts'. That is the most hellishly twisted scripture in the entire Bible.

> Isaiah 55:7 *Let the wicked forsake his way, and the unrighteous man his thoughts: and let him return unto the LORD, and he will have mercy upon him; and to our God, for he will abundantly pardon. ⁸ For my thoughts are not your thoughts, neither are your ways my ways, saith the LORD.*

When I was about 7, I attended a Sunday school where we were sweetly and without mincing words taught that Jesus used to smoke marijuana. And how he forgot to assist a fellow smoker who was in dire need of smoking. When Jesus realized that He had not assisted a fellow smoker He quit smoking and cursed marijuana. What you are taught at Sunday school is nothing but holy truth. And what amplified it was the word of the elders. Some elderly people told us it was so. I grew up believing Jesus used to smoke like a two storey building on fire! But something was not right somewhere. It used to ring in my little head all the time. When I became of age I began to read the Bible for myself.

Decades have passed. I have found the same problem recurring in another form. People would tell me Keyworth God's ways are not your ways His thoughts are not your thoughts. They gave me the scripture I believed it. For a while. I read the context it's totally different. Never let old wives fables keep you down. Go back to the scripture above. The Lord is talking about the wicked! See verse 7. The wicked should forsake his way and the evil person his thoughts. **Are you the wicked who should forsake his way and the unrighteous man who should forsake his thoughts?** If not, why do you appropriate what is the wicked's as your own? You are born again. God's ways are your ways. His thoughts, His Word are your thoughts. Friend what happens when the wicked forsakes his way? Correct. He follows the way of God. You are not the wicked. Do not accept a false image of yourself that is what Satan wants for you.

Psalm 37:23 *The steps of a [good] man are directed and established by the Lord when He delights in his way [and He busies Himself with his every step].*

(AMP)

Who orders your steps John, the devil? Nay. The Lord. He delights in your way! In fact He makes it His business!!!

Psalms 128:1 *Blessed is every one that feareth the LORD; that walketh in his ways.*

Psalms 10:4 *The wicked, through the pride of his countenance, will not seek after God:* **God is not in all his thoughts.**

(Emphasis added)

I attended a marriage seminar. The Bishop was teaching us on Successful Marriage. Being someone who had just come into Zambia, (you know how we behave when there's someone from abroad) we were ecstatic. He taught nicely until he said,

'Marriages are weak, and demons attack them very much because the couples live in sin. How can a husband see the nakedness of the wife? Or the wife see the nakedness of her husband? Believe it or not, I knew I wasn't hearing him properly .

During the Question and Answer session, I told him that what he had just taught was not biblical. *Young man, I have been in ministry longer than you.* There is nothing wrong with you seeing the nakedness of your partner! Some people are moving around, trying to make life miserable for couples. Marriage is under siege. We need to open our eyes. The devil has done all he could to change family as we know it. Such teachings that say seeing your partner's nakedness brings demons in your house are unbiblical. Come on, that is false holiness. See your partner's nakedness, enjoy yourselves. Your father in Heaven, Jehovah has blessed you with it. This mechanical sex in marriage the devil is introducing must be stopped!

Some people have been so tormented by Satan in their relationships to the point they want to just try it outside. What is outside is now more appealing. Why? Christian couples have been tricked into a lot of sexual endurance! There are many terrible teachings

on marriage. And don't let anyone tell you that sex is just for procreation. That is a fat lie! Some Christians because of age, spiritual maturity, actually think when they have sex with their spouses they become unholy. They can't express anything even in words because they fear to be defiled. Sex in marriage does not defile you! It doesn't. Where did you get that thinking from, is Satan your uncle? Which position is holy? I am not an expert on positions, but the best position is one that satisfies both of you! There is one position that I believe even God doesn't favor though. The tree position. Couples who have had sex in trees have lived to experience gravity working against them! People have ended up in hospitals, not to give birth but to have their limbs attended to.

Do I scream? Well, there is nothing wrong with it. One lady started screaming the name of a boyfriend and the love session turned into a punch line affair. Blows started raining. Unfaithfulness has lousy timing and a strange way of coming out. She forgot she was with her husband and thought she was with the boyfriend, the man she had been committing adultery with. The husband didn't waste time remembering his boxing moves. God does not condemn sex in marriage! Hebrews 13:4. **Sex is one of the perfect gifts from God.** *But pastor we marry because of lust.* Thank you for speaking for yourself. We do not marry to feed lust. **We marry because it is a gift from God! 1 Corinthians 7:7.** Let's point out something. Unless we point out specific examples of wicked ways and thoughts, many will still be in darkness about the meaning of Isaiah 55:8. We take a look at sex, for this is the center of the kingdom of darkness. Sex is good, and couples should do their best to make each other reach orgasm. But orgasm does not make you very holy. What am I saying? In the occult, they believe orgasm is the highest form of worship. It is the union of man and God. It's intercourse with God. Our friends in the other camp have been taught that to become very strong in the inner man, have constant orgasms. They devise ways of getting these ritualistic orgasms. **And one thing has baffled me (very few things shock me), how does one lick the anus of the partner to reach orgasm?** Seriously how does **rimming (that's what they call licking the anus)** give you orgasms? **Some will actually tell the partner to defecate. And when they do, they place their member in the feaces to get the much needed orgasm.**

Keyworth, you are a mental. That can't happen!

I also really wish it **doesn't** happen in society.

But what even makes it world record breaking is when one cannot have an orgasm until he or she eats the feaces of the partner!

Keyworth? Swear this is true.

Dear, I swear upon you this is true!

What has eating feaces and washing it down with some *ice-cold glass of* **urine to do with sex, anybody help me understand?! Coprophilia. And how it is spreading among our sweet icons and the young adults! Hmm.** A man was found in bed with a dog. The wife couldn't believe her eyes. Well, for some reason or the other she decided to forgive him. *Whoa. Where there is money, forgiveness comes naturally.* But the man looked at the wife, then at the beautiful ruby lips of the dog and its angelic smile, long eye lashes, the juicy and wonderful hips, the breathtaking eight or whatever number of breasts and the well manicured paws, he shook his head and told the wife, " Am divorcing you! **I want to spend the rest of my life with bingo.'** *(Half of the dogs in Africa are called Bingo!)* He was convinced the lady (dog) was a TOOT, (**Te**n **O**ut **O**f **Te**n). A total package of a partner! Yes people divorce, for stupid reasons mostly, but this one tops the chart. This is Guinness material.

Does that make sense to you? Divorcing someone to have **'an affair'** with a dog? I love the way we call sin today, 'an affair'. I am sure when he looked at the beautiful *feet* of the dog in slippers; he just shook his head and exclaimed 'That's my girl!' Weird. As you read this, there are strange policies being pushed to legalize incest. One girl in her twenties audaciously said, 'Daddy has told me I am sweeter than mummy. He doesn't find mummy good anymore he just sleeps with me.' I will spare you the gruesome descriptions of real sadism. Not the sweet side you may know. It is real hardcore horrendous evil. Ever heard of the black widow spider? The spider that devours its mate after mating? That's the picture of real masochism and sadism! **Is this sex as God**

intended? Or is there another god at work? **Isis.** The goddess the whole world has gone after. What does the Bible say about *her*?

> Acts 19:26 *"Moreover you see and hear that not only at Ephesus, but throughout almost all Asia, this Paul has persuaded and turned away many people, saying that they are not gods which are made with hands.* ^{27} *"So not only is this trade of ours in danger of falling into disrepute, but also the temple of the great goddess Diana may be despised and her magnificence destroyed, whom all Asia and the world worship."*
> (NKJV)

Do not take this demon lightly. The Bible says **whom all Asia and the world worship**. Many are under this demon's grip. And they are doing it willingly and stubbornly.

> Jeremiah 44:16 *As for the word that thou hast spoken unto us in the name of the LORD, we will not hearken unto thee.* ^{17} *But we will certainly do whatsoever thing goeth forth out of our own mouth, to burn incense unto the queen of heaven, and to pour out drink offerings unto her, as we have done, we, and our fathers, our kings, and our princes, in the cities ... and in the streets ...for then had we plenty of victuals, and were well, and saw no evil.*

The people, their presidents, businessmen and the clergy don't even mince their words. We shall worship Isis, who is referred to here as the Queen of Heaven. They have erected various structures to honor Isis. This sounds like a fairytale, but it is happening even in our days. **Whom do some of our leaders worship every July if not Isis, who is depicted as an owl on the US dollar?** Isis is Wisdom they claim. Of course, someone may argue, Keyworth it is Molech who is an owl. I agree the owl is Molech. But don't forget our friends have this male-female god. On one side the owl is Molech. On the other it is Isis. Is it clear, Dear? **Isis is Wisdom**. And they are panting for this wisdom. We may not like it but the world has gone after this sadistic, blood-thirsty demon. Is it not Isis we have chosen to honour by putting on our currencies and we blasphemously say in 'God we trust'? Isis, the owl on the US1 dollar, the goddess before whom the world is staggering has done great damage. It is shocking we don't seem to see it. In the scripture we read, the people have taken a stance. They say, '**It is more profitable to worship Isis. As for God we don't want to follow His Word**'. Fascinating. No wonder the occult is normal. Since the time is ripe for Horus (The one eyed Antichrist) to rule the world, what were deeper occult practices have been off loaded on the market. And the worst part, they have become normal. Why is it so? Most Christians don't know what or whom they serve. If you don't know your God, it is very easy to worship another god! Just because someone has said 'In God I trust' that does not mean you go and fall before his altar. His god, in whom he trusts, may not just be your god! Horus, who is the god of many these days has various names, one of them is **HARPO-CRATES**.

Egyptian religions of old (which have survived to our times and now envelope the world), would let women copulate with animals, goats, during fertility ceremonies to please the devil. Then their god would answer this worship. This is killing two birds with one stone. The first thing is that these women are promised sex, such as they have never experienced before. *Goats will drive you crazier than men*. Ha ha ha. Lunatics! But we are doing it even today. We are looking for ways of more cloying sex. Promises of intense sexual levels are being discovered and taught, and what do we call that? Tantric sex? Whatever. In the name of enjoyment, satanic rituals have been accepted. We put penises in mouths and lick vaginas and anuses. Milk shake has now been replaced with a glass of semen. Oral sex, we call it. But do we know that these are satanic rituals? I am not kidding. It is Satan worship. No wonder we exude little Christian power. How do we stand up against the enemy when we live according to his ways? It is these satanic rituals that have culminated into the erection of phallic symbols like obelisks and their female counterparts in many cities. Oral sex is about the worship of sex organs. **But that's just the tip of a huge iceberg.** We have been fooled. We are doing this in our Christian homes. Do we understand what is involved? Satan is just laughing at us. It's undiluted wickedness. Slow down. Read slowly. Oral sex is direct worship of Satan. At higher levels, experts, offer a prayer before doing it. In fact many are in a worship state as they perform Oral sex. **Yes, it is an undeniable fact Mike, that in occultism, the occult trinity (godhead) lives in three places in the human body and one of them is in the genitalia!** Christians are following a satanic ritual. Father forgive us.

AS YOU LICK, YOU ARE WORSHIPPING THE SATANIC TRINITY! *The things we do, out of ignorance...*God have mercy! The

devil is stupid. He makes us think we are enjoying ourselves, yet he is tightening his mangy claws on our souls. He is the winner in all this. Where is our benefit? But that is not strange if we look at some of our Bibles. Please read this scripture slowly.

Romans 8: 22 *For we know that the whole creation groans and labors with birth pangs together until now. ²³ Not only that, but we also who have the firstfruits of the Spirit, even we ourselves groan within ourselves, eagerly waiting for the adoption, the redemption of our body. ²⁴ For we were saved in this hope, but hope that is seen is not hope; for why does one still hope for what he sees?*

(NKJV)

Forgive my over working imagination. But when I read this scripture in the Message, I felt offended. Very offended.

Romans 8: 22 *All around us we observe a pregnant creation. The difficult times of pain throughout the world are simply birth pangs. But it's not only around us; it's within us. The Spirit of God is arousing us within. We're also feeling the birth pangs. ²³ These sterile and barren bodies of ours are yearning for full deliverance. ²⁴ That is why waiting does not diminish us, any more than waiting diminishes a pregnant mother. We are enlarged in the waiting. We, of course, don't see what is enlarging us.*

(The Message)

Look at the words being used here. While we see 'birth pangs' used in the first scripture, in the Message we see disturbing suggestions. What comes to your mind when you see **pregnant**, **The Spirit of God AROUSING us** within, then look at verse 24. **Pregnant woman, enlarged in the waiting**? What on earth is this verse trying to insinuate? I find it odd. Yes John, I understand. Arousing has various meanings. But look at the context in which it finds itself! Check the glossary Chapter 8—look at **tantra**. Is this what is meant here? What is enlarging about the pregnant woman? And then I read other portions. John 1:12 where it talks about the true self and child-of-God-self. What is **true self** and where does that phrase emanate? Is true self the same as higher self? Is it the same as divinity in man? Or is it the **core being** which the Message mentions in Matthew 10:28?

Esoteric teachings are now part of God's Word? Come on no one should think we are stupid and shove another gospel down our throats. **We have seen conspiracy theorists come up with wonderful discoveries.** Things that are mind blowing. **But a closer look at the solutions they offer us to fight against the satanic New World Order are even more mind blowing! The higher self, core being, chakras, pineal, tantra,**

kundalini, **The Bible is false, There is christ in every person just awaken him, Satan is love etc.** This takes you into deeper bondage! I mention this Destroyer–Doctor principle in The Mystery Of Lawlessness. *The devil is a smart fool.* **Anyone embracing or endorsing The Message is totally against the Lord Jesus Christ!** There is no middle ground. Period. The Message is full of New World Order phrases. We know what **true self** is all about. And where it really leads. **I am sorry but I firmly state, The Message, is total rubbish!** I have more than forty versions of the Bible. I am not against Bibles. But some have gone to evil extremes! **I have used the Message before, but what I have began seeing, is shocking.** A lot of things aren't okay in the Message, look at this. Compare these two scriptures.

> Mark 10:34 *And they shall mock him, and shall whip him, and shall spit on him, and shall kill him: and the third day he shall rise again.*

> Mark 10:34 *who will mock and spit on him, give him the third degree, and kill him. After three days he will rise alive."*
> (The Message)

Where does this guy get 'give him third degree' from? What third degree? We are being fooled here. Third degree has various meanings it's true. This is a direct play on our minds and the level of our intelligence! We are forced to assume the third degree he refers to is the common every day meaning, but looking at the whole Bible, it is pervaded with New Age references. So it cannot be the third degree we want to imagine. NEVER! *Good Lord, help us.* When are we going to start seeing these underlying messages? I've taken time to go through the Message, I hope you do also, and you will know if I am just bubbling. **The God of the Bible is god of green hope?** *I just can't stop falling in love with the Message.* **We know that both Osiris and Isis are worshipped as god and goddess of green .**

Enough is enough. Ignorance ends here. I am sure you have picked one or two secrets. The second benefit these women and men were promised, when you please the gods (The devil) he answers your prayer. See how satanic rituals are now part of us? And we are literally diving for them. All these things sound like fairy tales until we get a closer look and discover most of us, in our families, and in our bedrooms these things are happening. Are you doing any of these things? Please kindly keep away. Don't give the devil something he can use against you. How many people sleep with their relations physically and in dreams? Well, the poor victim will think it's a dream, when it isn't. Incubus and succubus. Fairy tales, huh? Don't play with Satanism. Don't. Divine science at work? As I have prayed for people I have come to realise that most victims have been attacked by their own relations. It is a host-parasite affair. **What most people call generational curses are sacrifices taking place every day! Yes most of the things people call generational curses are satanic attacks taking place right there and then. Someone is currently bewitching them.**

Evil has been underrated. Satanic sacrifice is not only killing, no. You can be a parasite. Pick a host, inflict various pains, after all, they cannot connect you to the misfortunes of the victim and your god answers your prayers. In fact this is the apex of Satan worship. To make everyone a host, one way or the other! Divine science. How cruel. But you can stand your ground in prayer. And make powerful decrees. The blood of Jesus does wonders, Satan knows this very well. Put on the full armor and fight like the child of God Jehovah you are! I discuss this Host-Parasite issue more in my next book "**ABIDE: THE KEY TO FREEDOM.**" The thoughts of the wicked are not like those of the righteous. You have just seen some examples of wickedness and thought life, and you know they are not like yours.

Proverbs 12:5 *The thoughts of the righteous are right: but the counsels of the wicked are deceit.*

The thoughts of the righteous are wrong?! Halleluiah. The Bible is sweet. Have you seen that scripture? Let us see ourselves the way God sees us. There is no excuse for having poor perspective after Jesus has come!

> John 12:46 *"I have come as a light into the world,*
> *that whoever believes in Me should*
> *not abide in darkness.*
> (NKJV)

Jesus has come to open our eyes. That's what the scripture is saying. **'Abide in darkness' means 'Living with poor perspective of life!' What do you see? Believe in Jesus today. Let Him open your eyes. When He opens your eyes you will understand someone orders your steps when you are born again.** Who orders your steps? God. Then how can your way be not His? Your steps are ordered by God and God Himself delights in your way. Common sense. How can God lead you and not delight in your way, which is basically His way? You are blessed. So what happens when the evil person forsakes his thoughts? Brilliant! He gets the thought life of God. God's ways and thoughts are part of this new person who, remember, is no longer wicked or evil because he is a new creation. This person now has the mind of Christ not the devil. The only ways he knows are those the Holy Spirit is leading him into. It is time to arise, God wants you to. And what does He say?

> Isaiah 55:5 *Surely you will summon nations you know not, and nations*
> *that do not know you will hasten to you, because of the*
> *LORD your God, the Holy One of Israel, for*
> *he has endowed you with*
> *splendor .*

The word splendor means glory. **Exploits** *is* your life style.

> 1 Peter 4:14b *...for the Spirit of glory*
> *and of God rests on*
> *you.*

Eva, the Spirit of splendor rests on you. People who know their God are strong and do exploits. Daniel 11:32. Are you strong in your faith? Do you know your God? I know my God and I know His ways and thoughts. I know what He says about me. And that is enough; I do not need a second opinion. In verses 12 and 13 of Isaiah 55 God reveals His thoughts and it is exactly what is said in Jeremiah 29:11. **In Philippians 4:8 God shows us how to think like Him.** He shows us how to think victoriously. That is your new thought life. If you think like that, your thoughts are His thoughts. We sometimes convince ourselves we are the devil incarnate and the next day we are the righteousness of God in Christ Jesus. What are we? Half devil half Jesus? It is time we left fables. It is time, your time to arise. Now that you know, the devil fears you. Jesus has been waiting for this moment. He is counting on you. And as friends in Christ we could share this little secret, **there is a ceremony for Overcomers**. See you there. After all, you have the best excuse for attending: It is your inauguration ceremony! Crowns are waiting for you. Attend without fail. Remember your vision is broad it is not just about you. You are blessed to bless. Reach out with the Lord's Word to somebody and change a life today. You can't keep this a secret. **Let's end with a strong admonition and encouragement.**

Isaiah 42:1 *...I have put My Spirit upon Him...⁴ He will not fail nor be discouraged...*

Do you know that because The Father has put His Spirit upon you, you can't fail? Discouragement is an option from the devil. It's for those who want it. It is foreign to our kingdom! GET UP! It is IMPOSSIBLE FOR YOU TO FAIL! The same anointing upon the Lord Jesus, the anointing that never fails is upon you! God will not fail. NO. Psalm 138:8 tells us that God will perfect that which concerns you and Philippians 1:6 Tells us

Philippians 1:6 *being confident of this very thing, that He who has begun a good work in you will complete it until the day of Jesus Christ...*

(NKJV)

Listen now, you have no excuse for not arising. There are a lot of things God has bestowed upon you. I am sure Satan has lied to you that you are insignificant. Know this and know it with all your being: **Nobody can do the job God has assigned you, better than you!** Believe it or not, you can't fail.

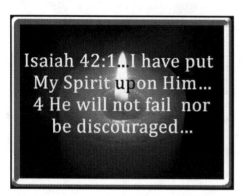

Isaiah 42:1 I have put My Spirit upon Him... 4 He will not fail nor be discouraged...

There is no 'I have failed in Christianity!' None. **The Greatest Generational Blessing in the universe runs in your life right now! God Almighty, Jehovah, the only true God has made an everlasting covenant with you. Isaiah 59:21. Enforce it!**

AFTERWORD

John 9:41 *Jesus said unto them, If ye were blind, ye should have no sin: but now ye say, We see; therefore your sin remaineth.*

BLIND, but claiming to see. In the end they pile damnation on themselves. Claiming to see, when one is blind is worse than being blind. When one is humble enough to have serious introspection, and come up with an unbiased conclusion, such a one has a good opportunity to know the truth. My heart is full of joy at the same time it is heavy. Some of you your eyes have been opened, for you are humble enough to accept certain things you didn't know. And from today, you will take a step in the right direction. But there are many, who claim to see but are totally blind, and because of that, the Master has decreed 'therefore your sin remaineth'.

Evil has taken a different turn today in such an astonishing way. I have mentioned things like oral sex, which we innocently find in our bedrooms not knowing, we are involved in satanic rituals. Blow jobs are a common thing. Nowadays you wouldn't call it sex without a blow job, would you? Those of you who have had the opportunity to read my book The Mystery Of Lawlessness will remember that the mark of the beast is already being given. How is it being given? Now is the time to remove our necks from the guillotines. A lot of evil has been unleashed and not everyone knows that they are being recruited to be part of this intricate Web of Death. Everyday where ever we turn, we find this evil beckoning. Evil is not always ugly. Sometimes it's sugar coated. And it tastes sweet for a while. And that is what has happened to many of the things we have acknowledged. We have evolution. Most people do not even know that there are two kinds of evolution we must contend with. The physical and spiritual. And that the so called Theory of Evolution comes from Cabala teachings. Sorcery is being taught in schools and we think we are getting *civilized* or educated. We even think we are *smart*. The party is on. Our joy is short lived. We seem to be enjoying ourselves as we party, not knowing that is just the way the script has been written. The wicked script writer makes sure we are focused on the wrong or trivial matters so that we don't have enough time to think about our lives seriously. He knows what lies ahead. Ahead, lies a great chasm, a chasm of hungry flames of fire yearning for our most prized possession, our souls. If we do not realise the danger we are in, destruction awaits us. People are preaching yoga 24/7 and its astral travel business. But they don't tell us that astral travel is demonic travel. The word 'astral' is from Ishtar or (you guessed right), Isis. Humble yourself before God and He will save you while you have the time.

Scripture shows God does not have a problem with people who humble themselves before Him.

> Isaiah 57:15 *The high and lofty one who lives in eternity,*
> *the Holy One, says this:"I live in the high and holy place*
> *with those whose spirits are contrite and humble. I*
> *restore the crushed spirit of the humble and*
> *revive the courage of those with repentant hearts.*
> 16 *For I will not fight against you forever;*
> *I will not always be angry. If I were,*
> *all people would pass away——*
> *all the souls I have made.*
> (NLT)

And none of us can claim to have a perfect walk. We are all striving. Our walk will always be perfected as we move on. But we must lay hold of the opportunity, while there is some time. With so much advanced wickedness, we must focus on Jesus. It grieves me to see such shocking ignorance among the people. Most of the Church does not know who the true God is. For whether we like it or not, there is a mixture today in our worship. And in some instances, outright satanic glorification.

The Mystery Of Lawlessness, my other book, mentions perhaps one of the biggest secrets that affect every human being alive today! You must know it. The Bible clearly reveals it, but most of us either ignore or the master of blindfolds has done his job to perfection. This secret, which is very prevalent, is found in the Book of Acts.

Knowing Jesus comes with humility before Him. Escaping the wicked claws of Satan needs a humble heart. Let the true Jesus alone guide you. For nowadays, we have many Jesuses, many Holy Spirits and many Fathers. It is only that sincere cry to God that will snatch us from the traps set before us. How many of us run around blindly for example with 'Xmas' tags? What is Xmas? Are we not clearly worshipping and praising Satan the archenemy of our souls? Isn't 'Xmas' honoring the All-Seeing Eye? **'Xmas' is another name for 'Satan mass'.** Just stick to 'Christmas'. *Keyworth what are you saying?* Dear Clement, you are the only one who is ignorant, everyone else knows. Let me share a vision I had a few years ago.

Excitement filled the air. People from all walks of life were in the auditorium. A huge crowd of people. This was a church gathering. But what puzzled me was that there was darkness in the church. The whole building was in total darkness. Then when I looked in front, to see who was leading, I saw Satan and he guffawed.

**'They think they are worshipping the true God,
but they are worshipping me.'**

Then I saw a few people exiting at the back. And at the back one could see light at the exit. This vision opened my eyes. Later, my eyes opened fully when the Holy Spirit took me on that six months *course*. I came face to face with a winged demon in radiant white! *It doesn't talk anyhow.* I wondered why the Holy Spirit had to show me this particular demon out of all those seemingly high ranking demons. I don't know why the Holy Spirit never told me who this was. Or my cranium was just super thick, He told me something a direct and astonishing clue, but it never registered. *When you are blind, you can't see an elephant a meter away.* It was many years later, it clicked; I had just met one of the most wicked demons in Satan's army, his deputy, Isis. This is not the time to be dull. This is not the time for some names. I belong to this, I belong to that. We worship like this, you worship like that. **Is what you are worshipping the truth? And will it lead to the salvation of your soul?** I have seen a strange design. The way religion has been woven. You can gasp! You freeze for a while. Isis is a serious Bible scholar and a genius Bible twister! We have the zeal, but no knowledge. Ladies and gentle men, we have been had! Wake up! Some people have discovered the deep wickedness going on around us. But I have seen a great flaw in them. Those who have certain insight about these wicked schemes are bitter. In trying to fight the wicked one by human effort, they find themselves enslaved by the evil one's bitterness. Others get trapped in another way. Those who study in their human intellect, find themselves dissecting the Bible. They pull this out, fix this in, that out. In the end, they are floating in the devil's cesspool. The wickedness that is there is astonishing. None of us can keep his soul. If you think you can hold on to that life and keep it, you are joking. You know you are joking.

People will feel offended because certain things they have regarded as dear, now have been labeled differently in this work. For example Passion of the Christ film has brought mixed feelings. Some have highly praised it. And why do they praise it? Because some religious person they respect told them so. Did they see it? Even when they saw the film, what they were told had already covered their faces. Judgement clouded. How unfortunate. When we tell them, about the esoteric messages there, they can't believe. Remember Elisha and his servant? Looking at the same thing, but drawing different conclusions? For example, what do you see when the tear falls from the sky and there is an earthquake? Shortly, when Jesus dies, what do you see? Many see Pilate. As for me I don't see Pilate. I see something else. I really believe it wasn't Pilate they wanted to show, but something in that room, which has a direct relation to death. **The scales!** The balance. In the occult there is a woman who carries scales. She is the one who metes out justice. In the occult, justice is a woman. A woman, who comes in many forms, but at the end of the day, we come to learn, is Isis. The scales allude to Isis the Mother god who weighs and judges the souls of people when they die! Is the Mother god, about to weigh the soul of this Jesus? **Friend, what do you see?** Perspective. If you do not have a clear understanding of things, you will find yourself in the middle of hell! Things are not what they seem. Things are not what they seem. Indeed. Is it a coincidence, that globally, justice is depicted as scales or a woman with scales? Biblical perception is your only key. Do not throw it away. Learn to view the world from the biblical point always.

There is a gospel, which has come. A Gospel that leaves people in excitement and comfort. Distracting them from knowing what is coming. Many of our spiritual leaders have taken this stance. Yes let's love. But a critical look at their love shows a demonic love. A love that denies Jesus and accepts evil ways. Anything that Jesus taught is attacked. What love are they talking about? The devil's love. How could someone who doesn't even know what love is, teach us? I am sorry, nobody will teach me love. Everything about me is love. Love is our life. I refuse to accept a poor concoction of love. Brethren, it's time to wake up. We must work out our own salvation with fear and trembling.

Search the scriptures and be prayerful. We are for signs and wonders. We are blessed. God has made a powerful irrevocable Covenant with us. A Covenant that gives us the ability to move in the demonstration and power of the Lord Jesus. His anointing is our anointing. His authority is ours. It's time we laid hold of that! You are a spiritual super commando. And it is required of every spiritual super commando to possess three crucial spiritual warfare instruments

✓ Spiritual Ears–– Revelation 2:7

✓ Spiritual Eyes–– Revelation 3:18

✓ Spiritual Mouth——Luke 21:15

Spiritual ears help you to be in touch with Head Quarters, Heaven. This also helps you intercept enemy communication. With spiritual ears you can easily avoid unnecessary spiritual ambuscades. We live in a wicked world. Darkness is everywhere. We need spiritual eyes. Every advanced army knows the importance of ENVGs——Enhanced Night Vision Goggles. Satan as a roaring lion loves hunting in the night, because the vision of most of his victims is impaired. Brethren, spiritual eyes (ENVGs) are a must for every spiritual commando. May the Most High God, open your eyes in the Name of Jesus. An army that just defends without attacking is a losing army. For you to be effective have that offensive instrument——Spiritual Mouth. Most curses come by word of mouth, decrees. You have the greatest offensive weapon, a missile that hits the target with unbelievable precision. Use that mouth and decree in the name of Jesus!

Evil has tried to twist scripture and leave us with a shell of the true Gospel. We won't fall for it. Every child of God who has been told he is unworthy because he is a sinner must totally reject this wicked Gospel. There has been a Passover.

> Romans 3:25 *whom God set forth as a propitiation by His blood,*
> *through faith, to demonstrate His righteousness,*
> *because in His forbearance God had*
> *passed over the sins that were*
> *previously committed...*
> (NKJV)

Have you seen it? **God had passed over!** Start afresh. That's God's message. They tell you how wicked you are. And how God has not forgiven you. Then they point you to what will make you be a better person without the help of the Lord Jesus. Madness.

Church, in us lives the **GREATEST POWER** above all powers! This is not about the false gods that are worshipped in the underworld. This is the true and only God. We can boldly say

1 John 4: 4 *Ye are of God, little children, and have overcome*
them: because greater is he that is in you,
than he that is in the world.

Rise to the occasion. You are of God. And have overcome! You are a warrior. As you rise know it may cost your life. It may cost you a lot. That is the price of following Christ. That is the price of truth. It is expensive. Truth usually costs blood. But we are bold. If you want God to come on the scene, be courageous. The miraculous will follow you. He will deliver you miraculously. But stand and defend the Gospel. Do something for Jesus. Death is nothing to fear. You have already passed from death to life. Why should you fear?

Enjoy the awesome power of the Most High in this generation. The many people you have read about, whom God used mightily, stood up in such a time as this. I am confident you are among those who like Paul, count everything as dung, to gain the Blessings of Jesus Christ. And Mordecai warned Esther, the same warning the Lord is giving you today

Esther 4:13 *And Mordecai told them to answer Esther: "Do not think in your*
heart that you will escape in the king's palace any more than all the
other Jews.[14] *"For if you remain completely silent at this time,*
relief and deliverance will arise for the Jews from another
place, but you and your father's house will perish.
Yet who knows whether you have come to
the kingdom for such a time as this?"

The blessings you have read in Satan's Best Kept Secrets are for the opening of your eyes. God has a lot more for you. Believe it or not generational curses are not for those who are born again. The Word of God is clear. **Every time one talks** about generational curses, they refer to the first Adam. And all the time, they suspend the work of Jesus. Observe that. All generational curses work on the principle that you are connected by blood. But this is what the Bible nullifies in

> John 1:12 *But as many as received Him, to them He gave the right to become children of God, to those who believe in His name.*[13] *who were born, not of blood, nor of the will of the flesh, nor of the will of man, but of God.*
> (NKJV)

You are not connected to the old blood of your father or ancestors! It is all about faith! And growing up! Grow up! You can't be a baby forever. Do not lead a careless life. Be prayerful. Satan and all his people hate praying Christians. That weakens demons. So the work of darkness cannot go very far. That's what brings about physical threats. You have defeated them on the highest level. The spiritual level. Prayer and decrees defeat the occult. Be careful not to be brought back into bondage. I repeat, generational curses were cleared by Jesus. We find it easier to blame demons of centuries ago, not the witch or wizard clad in an expensive designer suit next to you! Blind guides. **What did God promise us, in Jeremiah?**

> Jeremiah 31:29 *In those days they shall say no more, The fathers have eaten a sour grape, and the children's teeth are set on edge.* [30] *But everyone shall die for his own iniquity: every man that eateth the sour grape, his teeth shall be set on edge.*
> (NKJV)

The Bible is very clear. It's our heads that are not. So, if this is the case, what is really happening? We are being attacked by witches and wizards within and outside our families right now! Fight, the good fight of faith.

Success is your life style. Blessings unlimited await you. Light has shone on you. Your future has never been this bright with God on your side and Satan's wicked schemes and weaknesses exposed. **In the Name of Jesus, I decree as you respond to this Word courageously and joyfully**

- ✓ Numbers 6:24 **"The LORD bless you and keep you;**

- ✓ **²⁵ The LORD make His face shine upon you, And be gracious to you;**

- ✓ **²⁶ The LORD lift up His countenance upon you, And give you peace."'**

  (NKJV)

GLOSSARY

Chapter 1

Astral Travel: Also known as Astral Projection. The leaving of the physical body by the spirit into the spirit world.

Astrology: The mystical belief that the planets, stars, sun and moon affect individual's lives directly.

Bilocation: Being in two places at once. There is no biblical basis for this to happen to a Christian.

Born-again: The birth of a person by the Holy Spirit. The person dies to the first Adam's generation and begins living in the Second Adam's (Jesus) Generation.

Continuum Thinking: This claims there is no true or false perspective, it all just depends on how one looks at something

Cum: Semen or vaginal fluid

Evolution Theory: The theory popularized by Darwin which claims the purely accidental formation of species from common ancestral species to entirely different ones over long unknown periods of time.

HAARP: High Frequency Active Auroral Research Program. This programme has the capacity to produce a lot of good for mankind and extreme wickedness on the other hand. Drought areas could have rain. Earthquakes and tsunamis could be manufactured too.

Horoscopes: The charts used in astrology

Multi-location: Being in more than two places at once. This is very unbiblical.

Ouija Boards: Derived from two words 'Oui' French for 'Yes' and 'Ja' German for 'Yes'. Literally 'yes yes' boards. They are used for communicating with spirits.

Sorcery: The use of spiritual powers of darkness to manipulate people or things to ones advantage. Normally there is an agreement between the spirits and the person, what each party offers the other.

Transmutation: The ability to change one's nature into another

Yoga: This is a part of the vast world of eastern mysticism. The yoga varies. But it involves spiritual exercises and practices that seek to either help one know self better or unite a person with the universal spirit—Brahma. 'Yoga' means 'yoke'!

Chapter 2

Inviolate: God's quality or nature of being both Unapproachable and Indestructible. **1Timothy 6:16**

Omnipotence: Almighty or All-powerful

Omniscience: All-knowing

Chapter 3

Cauldron: A big pot with boiling liquid

Tyrannicide: The assassination of a tyrant

Chapter 4

Clairvoyance: The ability to see without the use of the optical sight, usually without respect of distance.

Word of Knowledge: One of the many spiritual gifts given by the Holy Spirit. Divine revelation of the past, present or future.

Clairaudience: The ability to hear things without use of the physical ears. Distance is irrelevant.

Chapter 5

HPT: Host–Parasite Technique. The system that the kingdom of darkness operates on. Demons need bodies to operate in, and every human being must be a host.

CAT: Counter Attack Tongues. Tongues that come when there is some impending danger. Though unknown to the speaker.

Chapter 6

GAOTU: Great Architect Of The Universe. Some believe 'Lucifer' is the Creator of the world. God has just hi-jacked.

Kamikaze: A term for Japanese suicide pilots in World War II

KNV: Keyworth Ngosa Version (There is no such version)

Occult: Means hidden or secret. This is a reference to the powers of the kingdom of darkness.

PAD: Personal Assistant Demon (This is meant as a joke)

Pederast: A nice name for a homosexual (gay) who has 'sex' with male babies.

Chapter 7

Chosen Generation: The generation of all those who are born-again, those who have been removed from the old Adam's generation into the last Adam, Jesus' Generation.

Clairvoyants: These are people with the 'ability' to see things without using the physical eyes. Clairvoyance literally means clear vision.

Crystal Meth: Also known as Methamphetamine. A stimulant and very addictive drug.

Curse: A prayer of a wicked man to a demon. It is also a declaration (confession) for a particular demon to attack someone or something.

I have referred to the curses coming from the devil and his children. God does not curse his children. For there is no condemnation to those who are in Christ. If God had cursed your family, before you became born-again, that curse cannot cling to you because of the blood of Jesus in your life now.

Hematidrosis: The strange and rare occurrence of sweating blood.

Kundalini Serpent: This is some supposed force in serpent (coiled) form found at the base of the spine. This force has to be awakened through certain practices and meditation. It has to go through 33 levels corresponding to the 33 vertebrae of the spine, from which we get the 33 levels of Masonic degrees. (It is imperative to know there are other shadow degrees above the 33rd degree).

Leviathan: A supposed name of an ancient sea monster, but used very much for Satan in the occult today.

Lying Wonders: Some things we see are magical illusions meant to throw our focus from the real issues.

Methuselah: The man who lived more than any other person. He went close to a thousand years—969 years.

Old Nick: A name for the devil

Palm Readers: Diviners or fortune tellers

Shroud of Turin: A linen cloth now kept in the royal chapel of the Cathedral of Saint John the Baptist in Turin, Northern Italy, believed to be the burial cloth of Jesus. It bears the image of a human face and features.

Soothsayers: A fortune-teller

Tarot Card Readers: One who uses tarot cards to tell the future or for meditation. There are various decks of cards used depending on the reader.

The Law of Excluded Middle: This law states that it is impossible for an object to possess a characteristic and at the same time not possess that characteristic.

Yoga: This is a part of the vast world of eastern mysticism. The yoga varies. But it involves spiritual exercises and practices that seek to either help one know self better or unite a person with the universal spirit—Brahma. 'Yoga' means 'yoke'!

Chapter 8

Chakras: The supposed points of power in the body

Coprophilia: The consumption of feaces and urine to get sexual pleasure

Esoteric: Secret or only understood by the *enlightened*

Incest: Sex between close relations

Masochism: The sexual pleasure derived from being inflicted with pain.

Oral Sex: Licking the vagina, the penis and the anus to give or get sexual pleasure.

Phallicism: The worship of sexual organs, believed to be the supposed place of residence for the underworld trinity. Today these monuments (phallics) are everywhere, showing us who is really being worshipped.

Pineal: This is a gland believed to be the third eye which sees in the spirit. Sometimes referred to as second sight or psychic

Rimming: Oral sex of licking the anus

Sadism: The sexual satisfaction gained from inflicting, usually inhuman pain upon another person.

Tantra: This is the system of raising the sexual powers in a person by using the Kundalini serpent. This sexual **arousal** grows until there is a union between the **god** and **goddess within** the person. Of course there are incantations (prayers) involved.

Tantric Sex: Sex that includes the worship of sexual organs and the discovery of better and deeper sexual satisfaction using religious power.

Third Degree: Rough interrogation. Also the third level of initiation in Masonic lodges the supposed highest degree. Apart from the bloodcurdling oaths, this degree is a *bit* innocent. The higher ones are horrifying.

PRAYER OF SALVATION

God I

believe Jesus is not a story,

He

is

real. He came on earth, He

died

that I might live. I believe He

died and rose from the dead by the

power of the Holy Spirit.

Jesus with my heart, my mind, my

mouth and everything in me I

confess you as my Lord and Savior.

Your blood was shed on the cross

for all my sins to be washed away.

I believe they are gone.

I ask you to come and live in me now.

I believe that by faith Jesus you

live in me. You are welcome. I'll live for

you now. Thank you I believe I am

now born again. In the Name of Jesus I pray. Amen.

YOUR NEXT BLESSING

ABIDE: THE KEY TO FREEDOM.

This could just be the key that unlocks that challenge that has plagued you all your life. Pastor Keyworth N. Ngosa unveils Satan's killer strategy for the family in the end times. This is the truth you hate to face, but if it's freedom you need, FACE IT! You definitely need this book!